i

First edition

Contents

CHAPTER 1

I Introduction

1.1 A Beginner's Guide to Medicine Interviews

The Basics

Medicine has long been one of the most popular university courses and consistently attracts many more applications than places available. This fierce competition is increasing year on year meaning that the medical school interview is now higher stakes than ever before. To deal with the increasing competition for places medical schools have developed new and innovative interview methods, such as multiple mini interviews, to ensure that only the very best candidates are selected from each applicant pool.

As you prepare for your interviews you may notice a variety of different interview styles being employed by the medical schools you have applied for. This can initially be difficult to navigate and may lead to confusion regarding how best to prepare when each interview appears to differ considerably. The key thing to remember is that regardless of how you are being assessed the main aim of the medical school interview is to ultimately demonstrate that you possess the qualities of a good doctor.

Understandably, the interview process is often the most anxiety provoking aspect of the entire medicine application process. This book has been put together by a selection of doctors and medical students to make interview preparation easier and more accessible for students across the world, regardless of academic background. We cover both, traditional questions and practical stations, as well as necessary background knowledge and tried-and-tested expert advice to score highly in the interview process.

Selection criteria

Every medical school publishes a list of selection criteria for applicants on their website. The selection criteria often echos interview mark schemes as it represents the qualities that each medical school is assessing applications for. Selection criteria can vary between medical schools so you should make sure to research each school you are attending interviews at.

The selection criteria for three medical schools is displayed below to demonstrate a handful of key potential differences.

Barts and The London School of Medicine

- Motivation and realistic approach to medicine as a career
- Show initiative, resilience and maturity
- Work well as part of a team
- Be well organised and demonstrate problem solving abilities
- Likely contribution to university life
- Communicate effectively in a wide range of situations

Hull York Medical School

- Understanding of current issues in medicine
- Insight   and   motivation   for   a   medical   career

- Critical thinking skills
- Personal qualities such as empathy
- Teamwork
- Tolerance of ambiguity and resilience

Southampton Medical School

- Self-motivation and resilience
- Evidence of reflection on relevant life experiences
- Can communicate effectively
- Understand the values of the NHS constitution

Disclaimer

Please note that the information above is valid and correct as of June 2022. This information is subject to change and so, we strongly advise applicants to consult the universities directly.

What are the interviewers looking for?

While selection criteria and mark schemes can differ between medical schools, often, the same skill set is being assessed throughout. The basis of a medical school's assessment of applicants is generally based on the skills listed in *'Duties of a Doctor'*, published by the General Medical Council. This document details the standards set by the GMC for all registered doctors practicing in the UK. A basic outline is reproduced below but it would be sensible to explore the document in full prior to your interviews.

Duties of a Doctor

Patients must be able to trust doctors with their lives and health. To justify that trust, you must show respect for human life, and you must meet the standards expected of you in four domains, described below.

Knowledge, skills and performance

- Make the care of your patient your primary concern.
- Keep your professional knowledge and skills up to date.
- Recognise and work within the limits of your competence.

Safety and quality

- Take prompt action if you think that patient safety, dignity or comfort is being compromised.
- Protect and promote the health of patients and the public.

Communication, partnership and teamwork

- Treat patients as individuals and respect their dignity.
- Treat patients politely and considerately.
- Respect patients' right to confidentiality.
- Work in partnership with patients.
- Give patients the information they want or need in a way they can understand.
- Respect patients' right to reach decisions with you about their treatment and care.

- Work with colleagues in the ways that best serve patients' interests.

Maintaining trust

- Be honest and open and act with integrity.
- Never discriminate unfairly against patients or colleagues.
- Never abuse your patients' trust in you or the public's trust in the profession.

During any medical school interview the above listed qualities will be tested in multiple scenarios. These domains represent the many soft skills expected of a trainee doctor, and medical school applicants are expected to reflect on their own experiences within the boundaries of these skills. We will explore how to achieve this in more detail in the "Personal Qualities & Skills" section of this book.

1.2 Types of Interview

Interview structure

The style of interview varies considerably between medical schools. Many medical schools now use multiple mini interviews (MMIs) which are broken into individually assessed stations, or "mini-interviews". However, some universities still use traditional panel interviews which take on a more conversational format.

You should try to establish the interview structure each medical school you have applied to uses so you can tailor your preparation accordingly. Please do bear in mind that universities have the right to change interview styles and structures between years, so information regarding previous application cycles may not be applicable to you. Ensure you read all communication directly from the medical school about your interview very carefully to ensure you know what to expect on the day.

Expert's Advice

Some universities may publish less information than others regarding their interview format. As this information can help tailor your preparations for that university specifically, anyone can request this information through the Freedom of Information Act. Make sure any request made is specific (such as number of stations, timing, inclusion of practical stations) and relates to previous application cycles only. This can give you a better idea of what the likely composition of the interview.

Multiple mini interviews

A MMI, or multiple mini interviews, consists of multiple stations which are individually assessed. Each station will require candidates to complete a task, such as take part in a roleplay scenario, or answer questions on a particular topic. Despite the difference in format, you will almost certainly still be asked traditional-style questions, such as those that explore your motivation for medicine and work experience.

Common Pitfalls

Do not fall into the trap of failing to prepare for these questions just because your interview is MMI style! While some question types, such as roleplay, are specific to the MMI-style you should also expect "traditional" interview questions to contribute a big proportion of your final score.

You are usually given reading time prior to each mini interview, during which you will be given a short brief that succinctly explores the foundations of the upcoming station. Once completed, you will immediately move to the next station in the sequence, until every candidate has completed the circuit. Typically, a MMI will comprise of 5-10 stations, each lasting for 5-10 minutes with around 1 minute of reading and preparation time. Notably, some universities do not offer any reading time, lending a unique challenge to candidates; ensure you are aware of this prior to the interview so that you prepare accordingly during mock interviews.

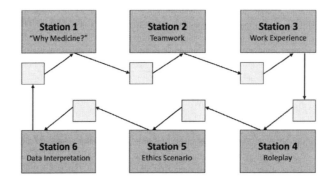

Your overall interview performance will be a collation of scores at every station. This can be used to your advantage as each interviewer is unaware of your performance at previous stations. Therefore, a poor performance in one question will not influence grading of subsequent stations. The key to success in an MMI is remaining calm and focusing on future stations - getting caught up on one poor performance may mean that you jeopardise showing your potential to the other interviewer.s

Panel interviews

A traditional panel interview is made up of a series of questions asked by the same interview panel. The interview is typically 20-40 minutes with a panel of 2-3 interviewers who may be clinical doctors, university academics, teaching staff or medical students. Some universities may even employ lay members of the public for these interviews to help assess a candidate's ability to communicate with the public.

This style of interview may feel more conversational. It is often far easier to establish and maintain rapport with your interviewers in comparison to a MMI due to limited time constraints. As the entire interview is conducted with the same interviewers, you can refer back to previous answers or experiences. The panel interview style tends to be less time pressured than a MMI, giving you longer to think about your answer or ask for clarification.

According the the Medical Schools Council published guide, *"Entry Requirements for UK Medical Schools: 2023 Entry"*, the medical schools planning on using the panel interview style are:

- **University of Cambridge**: typically two 25-30 minute interviews at one college
- **University of Glasgow**: two panel interviews lasting 30 minutes in total
- **University of Oxford:** typically four interviews at two different colleges
- **Queen Mary University of London**: one panel interview with two interviewers
- **University of Southampton:** selection day including 20 minute panel interview and group task
- **Swansea University**: three 20 minute panel interviews
- **University of Worcester:** semi-structured panel interview

Virtual interviews

In an effort to adapt to the changing world during the COVID-19 pandemic, many universities replaced their standard interview styles with virtual interviews. In the coming years we expect medical schools to revert back to in-person interviews however some may continue to make use of virtual interviews, particularly for international applicants. We will explore the added challenges of virtual interviews in greater detail later in this book.

Mixed interviews

Some universities may combine interview styles, using elements of standard panel or MMIs, but accompanied by other features. For example the University of Birmingham typically include a computer-based numeracy assessment during the MMI. Similarly some medical schools utilise group tasks, in addition to standard interviews, to assess the important skills of teamwork and communication style. We will discuss preparation for these types of interview later in this book.

1.3 Preparing for Your Interview

The medical school interview is the final hurdle to getting that all important offer and the thought of preparing can be overwhelming. While the remainder of this book will explore specific areas of the interview in depth, we have collected top tips from our interview experts which should be applied across your preparation.

Prepare for common questions There are some questions that are almost guaranteed to be asked at every interview, such as those discussing work experience and your motivation for studying medicine. Whilst it may be tempting, ensure that you do **not** over prepare or attempt to rote learn answers as this comes across as robotic and inauthentic. Instead, try planning out key points to mention and practice putting these points across in your own words.

Research the medical school You may be asked to explain your reasons for applying to a specific medical school and are expected to have a good knowledge of the curriculum. An answer referring to entry requirements or based purely on your chances of getting a place is unlikely to go down well. Instead, make note of the style of teaching and give reasons this style would suit you. Alternatively, there may be reasons that the location of the school is appealing or certain opportunities offered there that you're looking forward to. Universities want to see that you are excited to attend their particular medical school, not just that you applied because you had a good chance at obtaining an offer. We discuss how to answer questions about the medical school and curriculum later in this book.

Use the STARR technique to discuss your experiences When talking about previous experience, such as extracurricular activities or work experience, the STARR technique allows you to effectively structure your response and focus your answer without wasting time. The STARR structure is discussed in more detail in the "Work Experience" section of this book.

Research recent developments in the NHS and globally Interviewers will expect you to demonstrate an interest in healthcare by keeping up-to-date with relevant news stories. You may equally be asked for an opinion on a hot topic, for example changes to organ donation laws. These questions will be far easier to approach if you are already familiar with the topic being discussed and can draw on your existing background knowledge. Reputable and appropriate sources for medical school applicants include BBC Health and BMJ Student.

Practice verbalising your answers It might sound like common sense, but you cannot prepare for an interview by simply reading a book! You need to be challenging yourself and practicing your answers out loud. The best way to do this is practicing with someone else. This has an added benefit as you will also practice incorporating soft communication skills such as eye contact and body language. Alternatively, you can also record yourself responding to common interview questions out loud so that you are able to reflect on your own non-verbal communication skills; this is particularly useful for virtual interviews.

1.4 How to Use This Book

This book was written by a selection of doctors and medical students who have successfully interviewed at, or sat on interview panels of, some of the top medical schools in the UK. With our collective experiences, Medic Mind wishes to create an interview resource that students can use to practice questions and feel more confident stepping into the interview room.

Throughout the book you will find three types of text boxes with extra material. An explanation of these text boxes can be found below.

Expert's Advice

Here, our medicine interview advisors explain key pieces of advice that candidates may use to better their performance in their interviews. Often, the content of these boxes is what will help distinguish between the good applicants and the best ones.

Timing Tip

As the name suggests, these learning points refer to strategies that can be used to circumvent the strict time pressures of the MMI. These have been strategically devised to aid applicants in overcoming one of the greatest challenges in the UCAT - time - without sparing a single mark.

Common Pitfall

Our final focal point discusses the most common mistakes that applicants make at interview. Through years of successfully tutoring students like yourself, our experts have constructed a roster of much-needed fixes to commonly encountered problems. We strongly suggest reflecting on these points to avoid making the same, or similar, mistakes yourself.

The following chapters form the core content of the book, with information, answer structure advice and practice questions. As you progress through this book you will find many chapters contain *Sample Responses* and *Practice MMI Stations*.

Sample Responses

This section contains responses to a sample interview question related to the topic covered in the corresponding chapter. There are examples of both strong and weak answers, with feedback to highlight the key aspects to focus on. When reading this section, consider each sample response and decide if it is a strong, average or weak answer. Make a note of **why** you scored each answer they way you did and compare this to the written feedback given.

Remember any worked answers given in this text are **not** the only good response. We intended the model answers to be used as a guide to help structure your own response based on your own unique life experiences. Every answer you give should be personal to you and demonstrate your own personal motivations. It would be a good idea to start an interview notebook and create bullet point lists of how your would   approach   each   question.

Practice MMIs

The Practice MMI sections are intended to replicate a station during a MMI-style interview. The questions will be followed by a loose mark scheme. The best way to make use out of these sections is to have a go at saying your answer out loud, either on your own or with someone else, and compare this to the mark scheme. While the mark scheme is not designed to be exhaustive, it should give you a good idea about how to structure your answer and identify any key points.

Ultimately the aim of this handbook is provide medical school applicants with a guide to interviews containing the information that once helped us all pursue our dreams. We hope that you find it helpful and look forward to welcoming you as colleagues one day.

Good luck!

CHAPTER 2

II Motivation for Medicine

2.1 Introduction

The one question that is almost guaranteed to feature in any medical school interview is those that explore a candidate's motivations to pursue Medicine. It may seem clichéd but there is good reason for interviewers to explore your intentions. Becoming a doctor is a huge undertaking and medical schools have a responsibility to only select students with a genuine interest and understanding of the career. Exploring your motivations and understanding the reasons you are here is a key aspect of the interview so it is important to have something prepared.

Your answers to this section of questions will be personal to you. There are no right or wrong answers and it is important to fully reflect on your own motivations before beginning to draft an answer. Whilst we cannot draft answers on the behalf of candidates, we will explore tips and techniques to help structure a well-received answer as well as ways in which to explore personal motivations in a clear and structured manner.

Commonly asked questions

When exploring your motivations for a medical career directly, interviewers will often ask several follow-up questions. Assessors are looking for candidates to demonstrate that they have a realistic understanding of the career and that they have made an **informed decision** by considering both, the positive and negative aspects of the profession.

Example follow-up questions may include the following.

- If you are interested in science, why not become a laboratory scientist or researcher?
- Why would you want to be a doctor over a nurse or other member of the healthcare team?
- What do you wish to achieve in your career, outside of clinical practice?
- Are there any aspects of a medical career that you are not looking forward to? How would you manage this?
- What steps have you taken to explore or further your interest in medicine?

Common Pitfall

It is important to read the underlying intention behind the question being asked. For questions about your motivations for pursuing medicine, often an interviewer is looking to see if a candidate understands what they are getting into, speaks of both the positives and negatives and gives a realistic expectation of medicine as a career. Try to understand why a question is being asked and tailor your answer to this.

The key point to remember when answering questions about motivation for medicine is that it is not clear cut. While it is important to have a well prepared answer, you should be prepared for interviewers to scrutinise your response with follow-up questions. Whilst you are preparing your answer, try to anticipate areas that interviewers may ask you to expand on in more depth and prepare for this.

2.2 Why Medicine?

It is very likely that this question will be asked at some point during your interview. It is important to consider your genuine motivations that have driven your decision to apply to medical school. Your answer should be personal to you.

Simultaneously, medical schools are looking for candidates to demonstrate a passion or genuine interest in medicine, as well as a realistic understanding of the career. Therefore, your answer should be a balance of these two ideas, with specific examples from your work experience to evidence your argument and demonstrate insights you have gained. The interviewers want to see that you have thought about and carefully considered the career prior to applying.

Building an answer

While there is no set list of "correct" arguments to mention, the following points may help formulate a starting point to your answer.

Scientific or academic aptitude Studying Medicine is based on a fundamental understanding of human biology and biomedical sciences. Particularly in the early years of medical school, much of your learning will be centered around developing an appreciation for the anatomy and physiology underpinning clinical practice. Having a strong interest in science is expected of medical school applicants, and so, it is not a unique selling point in telling your story to your interviewers. Rather, reflect on the source of this interest. Consider projects, experiments and courses in school - or elsewhere - that sparked a passion for science and delve into this, instead of simply stating an interest in science.

Expert's Advice

Reflection is a key component of a good medical interview answer. When it comes to motivation for medicine, consider the ways in which early interests shaped your professional pursuits and may continue to impact your career moving forward. For example, simply stating that a case study into diabetes sparked an interest in healthcare will not garner as much interest as exploring the ways in which an understanding of endocrine medicine has shaped potential interests moving forward in your career.

Altruistic desire Being a doctor, like most healthcare professions, is ultimately a caring role. It is this aspect of healthcare that separates it from other scientific professions. What is it about this that appeals to you? Perhaps you enjoy the rewarding nature of helping others or have had previous caring responsibilities which would be good to explore here. Once again, focus on exploring these motivations as opposed to simply stating them; do so with structured examples, anecdotes and more!

Working in a diverse team The modern doctor rarely works in isolation. Good patient care stems from group effort involving doctors and other members of the healthcare multi-disciplinary team, incorporating many individuals with unique experiences and skills. Even among doctors, you will be expected to work with colleagues across different specialties and levels of seniority. Are there any examples where you have enjoyed or thrived working in a team setting? Delve into the qualities that make you both, a good leader and a good team player as these are both vital to a career in Medicine.

Challenging career The life of doctor is far from easy. A medical career will pose academic challenges such as devising ways to communicate with non-verbal patients or diagnosing rare conditions. Additionally, Medicine is intellectually, financially and socially challenging. If this challenge appeals to you, make sure you convey this to your interviewers using examples!

Expert's Advice

Focus on communicating a healthy attitude towards challenges and personal growth in your interview. It can be tricky to tow the line between appearing arrogant and coming across as under-confident or easily stressed by a challenge. Reflect on your own experiences to help convey a willingness to be challenged and to learn from your own mistakes.

Varied career Diagnosing and treating patients is only one part of the duties of a doctor. There are also opportunities to get involved in teaching, research and management. You might also be looking forward to learning about a wide variety of specialties at medical school where you will have the chance to try everything from surgery to psychiatry. If you have spent time shadowing a GP, think about the variety of patients and cases seen in a single morning. Is this something you could reflect on and incorporate into your answer?

Timing Tip

Remember that, particularly in MMI stations, you are under a time pressure. There are often follow-up questions that need to be answered within the time limit as well. Aim to include 2-3 well explained and detailed points, rather than simply listing multiple arguments without any depth. Answers that prioritise quality over quantity will ensure that there is still time for the interviewer to ask all of their questions.

Sample responses

> **Example 1** *"I want to do medicine because it is a very prestigious job and will allow me to challenge myself academically as I constantly strive to be the very best in what I do. Additionally, the opportunity to earn good money means I will always be financially secure."*

Feedback This is a poor answer. The student fails to mention anything specific to medicine and demonstrates no insight into the realities of a career in medicine. The overall impression given here is a candidate motivated by title, prestige and money.

Furthermore, there is little to no self-reflection into one's own abilities and skills nor a clear description of their initial inspirations and motivations. Consequently, an interviewer will not be able to glean an accurate portrayal of the candidate's intentions.

Common Pitfall

Interviewers will not be impressed by the mention of money or prestige in any answer to do with motivation for the career. There are many prestigious and well paid jobs aside from medicine so this answer suggests that a candidate is not motivated for the right reasons. Furthermore, it may unconsciously remove from the altruistic nature of the career by focussing solely on financial incentives and so, this must be avoided at all costs.

Example 2 *"I love the academic field of medicine, and it has been my dream to be a doctor since I was very young. My father had a life-saving operation when I was 16 which gave me an insight into the intricacies of hospital care, and the pressure-driven yet intellectually engaging environment of medicine."*

Feedback This answer is an average response. The student links lived experience to what they have gained by reflecting on their parent's illness and the ways in which this has influenced their career decisions. Whilst this personal touch is good, it risks coming across as idealistic given the use of words such as "dream" and "love". As a general rule of thumb, avoid mentioning childhood aspirations unless it can backed up with more recent experiences to demonstrate you have an understanding of both the pros and cons of the career.

Medicine is a complex career and so, childhood dreams and aspirations are rarely an adequate reflection of the profession as it is nearly impossible to know what medical practice entails at that age. If mentioning early experiences, ensure that this is described as an initial inspiration that encouraged further exploration through work experience.

Example 3 *"Over the past few years my interest in human biology has developed into a passion for medicine as I gained a greater understanding of the role of a doctor in the community. My work experience at a GP practice highlighted the importance of GPs as the first contact for patients in the community. Viewing the variety of cases the GP had to deal with, and seeing how they logically identified symptoms and asked questions to reach a diagnosis, showed me how medicine was an intellectually challenging profession that I would relish."*

Feedback This is a good answer. It links together two different, but equally important, sides of medicine - scientific theory and clinical practice. Including insights gained from work experience provides evidence for the interviewer and shows the student has been proactive. To further ameliorate this answer, the candidate can further explore the skills they have gleaned from this and other experiences that mimic those required for a successful career in Medicine.

Using evidence in your answer

Answering questions surrounding your motivation for studying medicine requires you to address two key concepts.

- **Passion for medicine** You should show that you genuinely are excited to study medicine and become a doctor.

- **Informed decision** You need to demonstrate that your passion for medicine is informed through work experience, research and spending time reflecting on the daily duties of a doctor to assess whether you are suitable for the career.

Importantly, your answers should show a balance of these two ideas. A person with a very strong passion for medicine but with little experience to justify this passion, or vice versa, is unlikely to be successful.

A good way to demonstrate both of these aspects is to use examples from your work experience to back up any points that you make. This shows the interviewer that you have reflected on your experiences and used this to guide your decision - a key skill for future doctors! Try to think of a number of examples that you could have on hand to reinforce your answers.

Expert's Advice

Once you have a good idea of how you would answer a question about your motivation for medicine, rehearse your answer with others to ensure you can explain yourself easily but do not sound over-rehearsed or robotic. Additionally, you can record yourself going over your response to watch back and critique your own communication skills. Hearing your answer played back can also aid you in picking it apart in a way that will mimick the interviewers.

Practice MMI station

Station brief: What inspired you to want to become a doctor?

Tell the interviewer about a patient you met during work experience or volunteering who inspired you to find out more about what was wrong with them.

Good answer A good answer may include:

- Interest in science, demonstrating a true passion for learning about the human body.
- Desire to help people, with reference to charity work or other examples illustrating a candidate's altruistic nature.
- Social aspect of medicine, with specific reference to the roles of patient contact and human engagement in a doctor's work.
- Work experience, showing insights gained during placements and how this has informed a decision to apply to medical school.
- Personal experience, such as a family member being unwell with reflections that support previous points.

Poor answer A poor answer may include:

- Unrealistic or idealistic motivations, for example "at age 7 I broke my arm and this inspired me to become a doctor".
- Superficial reasons that are unspecific to medicine, such as talking about a "desire to help people" without further reference to other aspects of medicine or linking to charity/volunteering work.

2.3 Realities of Becoming a Doctor

Medical school interviewers are looking for candidates to have a realistic understanding of a career as a doctor, including the challenges. You need to show an awareness of both the pros and the cons as interviewers will often ask you about both sides. The list below is not exhaustive but should help you begin to think about the arguments to include in your response.

Advantages of a career in Medicine

- **Immense job satisfaction and gratification.** Being a doctor gives you the ability to go to work and help patients at a personal level, truly making a difference to people's lives.
- **Academically challenging career with life long learning.** Throughout your career, you will constantly be using your academic skills to improve your knowledge and apply this to cases in front of you.
- **Able to combine science with altruism.** Medicine not only allows you to understand and apply science at a high level but relies on drawing upon your social and communication skills on a daily basis.
- **Well respected and stable career.** Generally, medicine is respected within society and offers a career that is sought-after, always needed and hard to replace. This lends lifelong stability.
- **Opportunities for self-development.** Treating patients is not the only aspect of a medical career. There are numerous opportunities for a doctor to develop their skills, be it through research, teaching or something completely novel!

Disadvantages of a career in Medicine

- **Stressful lifestyle with long hours, night shifts and lengthy training pathways.** This can lead to tension among family and friends who may not understand the nature of the work. It can also cause mental and physical burnout.
- **High pressure environment** where every decision counts and mistakes may have irreversible consequences.
- **Rude or disrespectful patients.** Unfortunately, this is inevitable as humans are unpredictable by nature. Furthermore, liaising with people who are upset, stressed or in pain will often lead to unfriendly interactions. Doctors are constantly under public scrutiny and in some cases, this can lead to complaints, even in situations not under your control.
- **Emotional impact on yourself.** Not every patient you meet will get better despite your very best efforts. While this is an acknowledged fact of medicine, it can be hard to deal with.

Expert's Advice

When mentioning the negative aspects of medicine an excellent candidate would also consider how they would personally cope with such challenges. By doing so, a candidate shows initiative and insight into their own capabilities. For example, when mentioning the high stress faced by doctors you could discuss how you plan to relax and handle pressure while at medical school.

Approaching questions about positive and negatives

The key to answering questions about the positive and negative aspects of medicine is to remained **balanced**. You should not come across as overly positive as this gives a naive and unrealistic impression, suggesting that you have not considered the realities of life as a doctor. Likewise, an answer that is overwhelmingly negative paints you in a cynical light and can lead interviewers to question why you have applied.

Good candidates will draw on their observations and work experience to answer these questions. For example, if you have shadowed an A&E doctor, mentioning specific positive and negative elements of the placement, such as challenging patient encounters, demonstrates an ability to reflect and learn from past experiences. This conveys a level of engagement and self-reflection suggesting that you have partaken in the work experience to actively learn from it rather than to ameliorate your application.

When exploring the disadvantages of a career in Medicine, we strongly encourage that candidates discuss the ways in which to combat these challenges whilst conveying a level of personal resilience to showcase an ability to constructively deal with them.

Timing Tip

A useful structure when approaching questions about the realities of medicine is to give a positive, followed by a negative, followed by another positive and so on. This ensures a balanced response is put forward even if time runs out.

Practice MMI station

Station brief You are a final year medical student on placement in an A&E department. Your colleague, Deji, is feeling stressed out with his work. He has lost motivation for medicine and is tired of the negative aspects of the job. Speak to him about his concerns, address the points he makes and emphasise the positive aspects of his job as a doctor.

Notes for actor (Deji) You are frustrated as patients have been shouting at you due to long waiting times all day and this is not your fault. You are not enjoying A&E work as you do not get to know the patients well. You are finding the hours long and stressful and you haven't been able to spend any meaningful time with your partner for two weeks.

Good answer A good answer will:

- Take a balanced approach whilst still being realistic about the advantages and disadvantages mentioned. The role of a doctor is never glamourised but the tone is not overly negative either.
- Empathise with Deji. His concerns are valid and should not be dismissed. Good candidates will show him concern and offer support where appropriate.
- Mention non-clinical roles. As Deji is struggling with his clinical workload it is reasonable to remind him of other opportunities available to him as a doctor, such as getting involved in teaching or research.

Poor answer A poor answer will:

- Be unrealistic in the portrayal of medicine, either too positive or overly negative.
- Give generic advice, unspecific to the situation. In a roleplay scenario you need to respond to what the actor is saying. Mentioning pros and cons not relevant to the specific scenario demonstrates poor listening skills.
- Demonstrate poor communication. While this interview station is assessing your understanding of medicine pros and cons, you will also be assessed on your communication skills. Answers that do not empathise with Deji's concerns will not score highly no matter the validity of the points made.

2.4 Roles of a Doctor

Being a doctor in the 21st century is more than just diagnosing illnesses and prescribing treatments. A medical career is multi-faceted with multiple opportunities available to doctors outside of the clinical environment. Additionally, medical training enables you to pursue several different paths, allowing doctors to tailor their career to their own personal interests alongside clinical work in the specialty of their choice.

Showing an understanding of the variety of roles available in medicine demonstrates you have fully researched and considered life as a doctor and that you have made an informed decision about your own career. This in turn supports your motivation for medicine as you can reflect on your experiences to show suitability and excitement for multiple aspects of a medicine. While reading the roles of a doctor below, consider which non-clinical roles you may be suited to and if you have any experiences - such as work experience or extracurricular activities - that demonstrate this.

Expert's Advice

Reflecting on potential career interests and how these can be pursued whilst at medical schools gives an interviewer an idea of what you can bring to that particular institution. You may even want to research which areas of medicine each university is particularly known for and relate this to your own personal interests. This demonstrates commitment and consideration of long-term career foals.

Clinical practice Clinical practice refers to the act of treating and caring for patients. This is often seen as the primary role of a doctor and involves various activities such as interpreting investigation results, communicating with patients and deciding on treatment plans. The majority of doctors will be involved in the clinical management of patients to some degree, although it is worth remembering that some specialties, such as radiology or public health, may have relatively few direct interactions with patients. Within clinical practice, there is a range of roles, from acute care in emergency departments to long-term care in primary GP centers.

Management There are multiple opportunities for doctors to become involved in business and strategy within the NHS. Doctors are vital to making the NHS a more efficient system and can lead the development of new services. You may have even met a GP partner during work experience - these are GPs who have invested into the practice and have a large degree of control in the running of the GP practice as a business. Alternatively, if you have previous leadership experience you may reflect on this and consider how these skills could link to a career incorporating management.

Teaching All doctors have to act as teachers to some degree, be it through supervising junior doctors or explaining a complex disease process to patient. There are also many additional opportunities for doctors to become involved in medical education and formally teach medical students or junior staff at medical schools across the country. Consider the skills required by those in educational roles and how these may be demonstrated   within   the   context   of   your   own   experiences.

Research Healthcare provision in the UK is "evidence-based", meaning that all clinical interventions are based on robust research studies supporting their use. As such, medicine can only advance if there is a consistent and robust effort towards scientific advancement and research. Many senior clinical doctors work alongside academic staff to conduct experiments to further their particular fields. You can begin to get involved in research as early as medical school if this is something that interests you. You can demonstrate an aptitude for research at your medical school interview by discussing additional study in a topic of personal interest, such as an EPQ, summer project or IBDP dissertation. Even simply attending a free virtual course in an area of interest can act as strong evidence of a commitment to research.

Charity and volunteering work There are many medically-related charities that rely on the support of doctors to continue their valuable work. You may have even begun volunteering already and can draw on these experiences to reflect on how valuable your skills can be in this sector.

Military practice Doctors are required to provide front line medical support for the armed forces. A degree in medicine opens the door for you to enter the services via this route and use your unique skill set to serve the country.

This list is not exhaustive as the opportunities available to doctors are diverse and constantly evolving. There are many additional opportunities such as health technology and informatics, health economics, policy making and public health to name just a few. If you have an interest in a particular field, conduct some research and consider how this could be incorporated into a medical career.

Sample responses

What do you wish to achieve in your career in medicine, aside from clinical practice?

Example 1 *"I would like to master a particular type of surgery, as it has always been a goal of mine to become a high level surgeon. While I was on my work experience placement, I was lucky to talk to a surgeon who spoke about his own private work. Therefore, when I become a consultant I look forward to opening a private practice and having more of a management role as well."*

Feedback This is a poor answer. While the student attempts to reflect on their work experience, they do so superficially and only identify opportunities in the private sector. This comes across as money motivated and shows a lack of insight into management opportunities, both in the NHS and at more junior levels. Furthermore, there are no links to the candidate's own skills to evidence their career motivations.

Example 2 *"I hope to become involved in academic research alongside my clinical career. During my work experience placement at a GP practice, I met a patient who was taking part in a clinical trial which highlighted to me the important interaction of biomedical research and patient care. While researching your medical school, I was particularly excited by the opportunity to take an intercalated research year during the medical degree as this would explore my research interests further and gain valuable experience."*

Feedback This is a good answer. The student identifies a suitable area of non-clinical practice and demonstrates an understanding of why research is important. The student also shows initiative by having plans to become involved in research early in their career. Notably, the candidate mentions opportunities to do so at the medical school in question which echoes a sense of commitment to researching potential career pathways   and   opportunities.   This   will   be   well   received   by   interviewers.

2.5 GPs, Surgeons and Hospital Doctors

There are currently over 100 specialties and sub-specialties recognised by the General Medical Council. As a medical school applicant, you are expected to have a broad understanding of the different specialties that doctors can work in and to have thought about where you see yourself working. In general, doctors can be split into three broad categories - GPs, hospital doctors and surgeons. There are, of course, specialties that cross or do not completely fit into these categories but splitting the specialties in this way forms a useful starting point for discussions.

General practice

General practitioners (GPs) treat common medical conditions and refer patients to hospitals when specialist care is needed. They are usually the first point of contact for patients in the community. When a patient develops a medical problem, such as a breast lump, it is the GP who initially assesses and decides if a patient needs to be referred urgently. They are also a central point of contact for those with chronic health conditions. The GP sees a patient holistically and is able to take input from multiple specialties to provide an overarching and continuous treatment plan.

Why would you want to become a GP? Points you may wish to mention in your answer include:

- **Holistic approach** to patient care as a GP considers the psychological and social aspects of a patient's life alongside their clinical care.
- **Continuity of care** as GPs are a long-term point of contact - some patients remain with the same GP their whole life!
- **Variety of presentations** as GPs are generalists meaning they deal with cases spanning virtually every specialty and age group.
- **Flexible hours** compared to other specialties, with a lack of night shifts and relatively little "out-of-hours" or "unsociable hours" work.
- **Entrepreneurial** element including management of GP practices by becoming a GP partner.

Hospital doctors

Hospital doctors are usually specialised into a particular field, from emergency medicine to cardiology to paediatrics. Hospital doctors treat patients who have been admitted or referred to hospital for specialist care. Typical activities of a hospital doctor involves leading ward rounds, running outpatient clinics, ordering and interpreting specialist tests and offering advice to doctors in other specialties. A **physician** is used to describe a hospital doctor who prefers medical treatment of patients rather than using a surgical approach. For example, a cardiologist may use drugs to treat heart disease whereas a cardio-thoracic surgeon would perform an operation.

Why would you want to become a hospital doctor? Points you may wish to mention in your answer include:

- **Intellectually challenging** as patients are referred when a GP is unable to manage a condition in the community, meaning hospital doctors typically see more complex cases.
- **Usually specialised**, leading to an in-depth level of knowledge and ability to select which patient groups you work with. For example, a neonatologist's patient group will be very different to a geriatrician!

- **Pathology orientated** approach, involving a deep understanding of the disease processes in your field.

Surgeons

A surgeon is a doctor who specialises in performing operations to repair, remove or replace a diseased or damaged part of the body. Surgeons often specialise in one area of the body and become highly skilled at the procedures they perform. As technology improves, surgeons are expected to learn and keep up-to-date with the latest advances in their field providing an opportunity to integrate modern technology into their clinical practice.

Why would you want to become a surgeon? Points you may wish to mention in your answer include:

- **Procedure orientated** involving complex practical procedures - ideal if you have strong manual dexterity.
- **Immediate results**, such as the instant improvement of symptoms following re-perfusion of the heart muscle after a heart attack!
- **Diverse role** including activities outside of the operating theatre such as leading clinics, reviewing patients on the ward and providing long-term post-operative care.

Expert's Advice

If you have taken work experience placements in different settings it would be useful to compare the day-to-day experiences of the different types of doctor you have observed. For example, how is being an A&E doctor is different to being a GP in terms of types of conditions seen, time spent with patients and access to investigations and treatments. This will show your interviewers that you have done more than simply attend; you have thoroughly analysed and reflected on your experiences to further define your own career goals.

What specialty?

Even though it may seem like a long way in the future, you may be asked about which area of medicine you are planning on specialising in during your interview. A degree in medicine will open many doors and it can be overwhelming, even for junior doctors, to decide which route to take. It is common for medical school interviewers to ask questions such as *"Is there a particular area of medicine that you are interested in specialising in?"*, which can throw off candidates who have not thought this far ahead!

Common Pitfall

It may be tempting to pick a prestigious or competitive specialty for your answer in an attempt to look ambitious. Interviewers are not assessing the specialty you choose to talk about. They would rather you speak confidently and clearly about a potential career in general practice backed up by work experience, over mentioning ambitions in neurosurgery without any insight or knowledge of the job.

It is useful to start by understanding why interviewers are asking this question. No one is expecting you to have firmly decided which area you would like to specialise in at this stage. Instead, interviewers are looking for candidates who are open minded, excited to explore the variety medicine has to offer and have a good understanding of the different roles available.

This question is ideal to bring in and show off the work experience you have completed. Regardless of which doctors you have observed, you can mention the positive aspects of their role to support your answer and show enthusiasm. If you are struggling, it can be helpful to use the broad categories of doctor to help frame your answer. For example, identifying if medical, surgical or primary care specialties are most interesting to you to begin with. This way you show you have thought about the future, and which direction you see your career going, but are not too narrow-minded by fixating on a specific sub-specialty.

Sample responses

Example 1 *"As I am at such an early stage of my career, I am currently unsure exactly what I want to specialise in. I will find out during medical school, as currently I do not know enough about each specialty for any particular field to stand out to me."*

Feedback This is a weak answer. While it is understandable that medical school applicants would not have a definite specialty in mind, this answer implies a lack of knowledge about the specialties available and comes across as apathetic and uninterested. There is also no mention of work experience or personal insight.

Example 2 *"I am determined to become a cardiologist due to the work experience placement I did shadowing a consultant cardiologist in my local hospital. Viewing the ward rounds, clinics and consultations inspired me and I am certain that cardiology is my true passion."*

Feedback This is also a poor answer. The student shows interest in a specialty but is so narrowed to a specific field, such that the candidate appears close-minded. Their reasoning for their interest - "ward rounds, clinics and consultations" - is not specific to cardiology and consequently does not support their interests as being genuine. This invites interviewers to ask some tricky follow-up questions around the subject, for example, "I am a respiratory consultant and I also conduct interesting ward rounds and clinics, why wouldn't you want to do respiratory medicine?"

Example 3 *"As I am so early in my career, I am mindful to be open-minded going into medical school as I am sure I will experience many interesting specialties. However, I do have a keen interest in the field of genetics and its application to medicine. Ever since the completion of the Human Genome Project, the specialty has advanced at a rapid rate and the idea of working with the latest technology is something that excites me. I would love to explore this during medical school, perhaps during the iBSc year that you offer!"*

Feedback This is a good answer. The candidate demonstrates an interest in a particular specialty and gives ideas for how they will develop this interest during medical school, showing initiative and drive. Furthermore, the answer is personalized to opportunities available at the specific university, which shows insight into the school itself and will come across very positively to the interviewers.

2.6 Other Healthcare Professionals

Who is part of the multidisciplinary team?

As a medical school applicant, you are expected have a basic understanding of the different roles within the MDT for both doctors and non-doctors. You may be asked about some specific roles or could be asked about the value of the MDT as a whole. The table below lists some of example roles found in an MDT, but bear in mind that each MDT makeup will be specific to the specialty involved and can vary between local areas too.

Role	Explanation
Consultant	Senior specialist doctor responsible for overseeing overall care of a patient
Junior Doctor	Doctor in training working under supervision of the consultant
GP	Co-ordinates care of patient within the community
Radiologist	Doctor who specialises in interpreting scans and reporting findings of other imaging techniques
Nurse	Oversees the day-to-day care of a patient
Physiotherapist	Help restore function through movement and exercise
Occupational Therapist	Support independence in daily life such as assessing patients for specialist equipment
Physician Associate	Support doctors to diagnose and manage patients
Speech and Language Therapist	Provide support for patients with difficulties speaking, eating, drinking or swallowing
Counsellor	Helps manage emotional impact of illness
Dietician	Provides nutritional support and advice about diet

Common Pitfall

When talking about other healthcare professionals some applicants are overly negative as they try to emphasise why they applied for medicine rather than other healthcare courses. Always remain respectful and complimentary towards other professions as interviewers are looking for candidates to be appreciative of the input of every member of the MDT.

Why medicine and not nursing?

One of the hardest questions to answer about your motivation for medicine is *"Why become a doctor instead of a nurse?"*. A lot of people interested in becoming doctors do so because they enjoy helping people and also like learning about how the body works - both of these elements are also present in nursing.

Furthermore, the roles of nurses and doctors are increasingly overlapping. For example, nurse practitioners can prescribe, undertake research, take on leadership roles and diagnose patients. In order to answer this question, you need to fully understand the role of a nurse and how this differs to the role of a doctor.

Two key points to mention are:

- **Ultimate responsibility** It is doctors who ultimately have responsibility and drive the decision-making process regarding a patients care. Nurses contribute greatly however the final decision rests with doctors.
- **Different challenges** Although there are some exceptions, such as nurse practitioners, in general a doctor's role places greater emphasis on diagnosing and prescribing than that of nurses.

Expert's Advice

If you have spent time with or observed nurses during your work experience placements this is a good time to mention it! Doing so shows the interviewer's that you have not simply dismissed the idea of becoming a nurse due to prestige and have an informed idea of the differences between nursing and medicine.

Your answer must tread the careful line of explaining why you do not want to be a nurse, while appreciating the brilliant work that nurses do and never undermining the role. Remember that some members of the interview panel may be nurses or other allied healthcare professionals - offending their profession is never a good idea!

Worked examples

Example 1 *"My main goal is to conduct research as I am really passionate about genetics and enjoyed me placement in a lab last summer. Sadly, nursing does not allow you to take a role in research alongside clinical work unlike medicine."*

Feedback This is a poor answer. It implies the student's main focus is biomedical research and questions their motivation for the clinical aspect for medicine. Furthermore, nurses can become involved in research activities (although it is still more common for doctors to do so) therefore this answer highlights a lack of understanding of the scope of a modern nurse.

Example 2 *"Nurses play a pivotal role in the day-to-day care of patients. I would enjoy the patient contact and human interaction involved in the nursing role, however I am drawn to the problem-solving aspect of medicine. The ability to diagnose, decide treatments and take the ultimate position of responsibility for a patient suits my academic ambitions more."*

Feedback This is a good answer. The student is complementary towards nursing and by highlighting aspects of nursing they may enjoy the candidate has avoided dismissing the career as an option. While some nurses are able to diagnose and prescribe, the position of ultimate responsibility is unique to doctors.

2.7 Extracurricular Activities

In this section we will discuss how to incorporate extracurricular activities into answers about your motivation for medicine. We talk about extracurricular activities and hobbies in more depth further in the book, but if you have undertaken activities that draw attention to your interest in medicine then it is a good idea to discuss them when this topic arises.

What extracurriculars should you mention?

When talking about your motivation for medicine, you need to demonstrate a genuine passion for medicine. If you can show the interviewers that you have actively taken steps to further explore any interest you have, it displays a degree of proactivity, dedication to the subject and motivation to learn.

Extracurriculars relevant to your motivation for medicine could include any of the following.

Research placements Some universities host summer schools allowing students to conduct short research projects in their labs. Alternatively, if you are a graduate applicant you could mention a research project conducted as part of your degree relevant to a particular area of medicine that you are interest in.

EPQ and other projects An EPQ is an additional qualification taken alongside A-Levels requiring the submission of an extended essay on a topic of your choice. If you have taken an EPQ in a medical topic, make sure to mention it and reflect on what you learnt. You may also have researched a particular topic in depth for another project such as an essay competition or science fair.

Attending talks There are numerous free in-person and online talks relevant to medicine and biomedical science. Take a look at your local university's outreach programme as they may conduct sessions aimed at applicants. You can also find many relevant pre-recorded lectures or podcasts online. Make sure you can briefly summarise the topic in 30 seconds as interviewers may want to check your comprehension!

Reading medical related books Every applicant should read at least one medicine related book before your interview. There are a plethora available across a broad range of specialties and you should be able to find many of the most popular titles in your local or school library. During the interview, make sure to reflect on what you have read and explain how this has influenced your decision to medicine. It is also wise to recap the book just before your interview by reading online summaries in case the interviewers try to catch you out.

Societies at school Your school may run a medical society aimed at aspiring doctors. If you have attended any sessions, mention that you are a member and describe the types of activities or workshops involved. If your school doesn't have a medical society, consider setting one up as this demonstrates great leadership skills!

Volunteering Any volunteering work taken in a healthcare or caring setting is valuable and demonstrates your commitment to medicine. Volunteering does not have to be in a hospital as the majority of volunteering placements   demonstrate   multiple   transferable   skills   and   dedication.

Worked examples

Example 1 *"As I have a keen interest in medical ethics and its application to clinical practice, I decided to set up a Medic Ethics Society at my school. Every week we discuss current affairs in the healthcare environment and the importance of being aware. One such recent discussion was on the changes to organ donation law."*

<u>Feedback</u> This is a good answer.

Example 2 *"Last year I read "With the End in Mind" by Dr Kathryn Mannix, which is a book written by a palliative care consultant exploring society's attitude towards death and dying. It made me think about how I would approach discussions about end-of-life care as a doctor, and how my preconceptions about death might influence these discussions. Consequently, I decided to arrange a two-day shadowing placement at my local hospice to further explore the role of palliative care in my own community."*

<u>Feedback</u> This is an excellent answer. This candidate has shown an interest in a specific area of medicine, supported by their decision to use their free time to conduct further reading about the topic. The student reflects on their reading and goes on to show how this has subsequently influenced their actions by arranging shadowing, demonstrating that they are learning from their experiences.

2.8 Practice Questions: Motivation for Medicine

1.   Why do you want to become a doctor?
2.   What sparked your interest in medicine?
3.   What are the pros and cons of medicine?
4.   Have you thought about which specialty you would like? What is it about this specialty that appeals to you?
5.   What are your main goals for your career in medicine?
6.   What other health professionals are involved in patient care? What do they do?
7.   Describe the role of a nurse. How is this different to that of a doctor?
8.   Why makes you want to be a doctor rather than a nurse?
9.   Why makes you want to be a doctor rather than a physician's associate?
10. If you couldn't be a doctor, what job would you do?
11. What would you do if you were rejected from medical school this year?
12. Describe an interesting recent medical development that you have read about.
13. When you think about becoming a doctor, what are you most looking forward to?
14. When you think about becoming a doctor, what are you least looking forward to?
15. What impact do you hope to make in the field of medicine?
16. Do you agree with the statement "medicine is a vocation"?
17. What is a particular aspect of medicine that interests you?
18. Would you rather be a GP or a surgeon?
19. Describe a time where a doctor inspired you.
20. Tell me about a medicine-related book that you've read.
21. What do you think interviewers should be looking for whilst interviewing?
22. How would you dissuade someone from studying medicine?
23. Why do you think people leave the medical profession?
24. Which medical specialty are you least interested in? Why?
25. What does a doctor do aside from treating patients?
26. How have you acted on your interests in medicine?
27. How has your work experience influenced your decision to apply to medical school?
28. What was your favourite part of your work experience?
29. Were there any parts of your work experience that you didn't enjoy?
30. Who is the most important member of a multi-disciplinary health care team?

CHAPTER 3

III Work Experience

3.1 Introduction

Work experience in the context of medical school admissions can be defined as any type of activity or life experience which has prepared you for a medical career in some way. Medical schools generally appreciate that work experience can be difficult to obtain depending on your personal circumstances, so the majority of schools do not require a minimum number of hours as part of their selection processes.

Common Pitfall

Remember that shadowing an NHS doctor is not the only form of valid work experience! A broad range of experiences including volunteering in a hospital or care home, paid employment as a healthcare assistant, virtual work experience programmes or placements abroad can all be used to answer questions referring to your work experience.

You will likely be asked about your work experience directly with questions such as *"What was your favourite part of your work experience?"*. However, this is not the only time work experience can be incorporated in your answer. It may be useful to consider work experience as **evidence** that you can use to strengthen most answers. For example, a strong answer to the question *"What are the challenges of working as a doctor?"* will use observations from their work experience to support any points made. Try and show off all the interesting work experience you have completed whenever it is relevant!

Why do we need work experience?

There are a number of reasons why medical schools ask applicants to carry out work experience placements, including:

- Gaining a **realistic** understanding of medicine, including the physical demands of the job, organisation of the NHS and emotional demands of a medical career.
- Developing values and skills essential to becoming a doctor, including communication, teamwork and empathy. We will explore this further in the "Personal Qualities and Skills" section of this book.
- Demonstrating motivation and commitment to a career in medicine, particularly applicable to long-term placements requiring a significant time commitment.

Keeping these three points in mind when talking about work experience at your interviews will ensure you are providing examples relevant to the competencies interviewers are assessing.

Using the STARR approach

Medical school interviewers are expecting candidates to **reflect** on their work experiences. Reflection is a key skill in medicine as being able to reflect on your experiences, both good and bad, allows doctors to learn from cases they encounter. You will be expected to produce reflective essays during medical school, so demonstrating good reflective practice at interview will not only allow deeper discussion of your work experience, but may convince the panel of your suitability to study medicine too!

The STARR approach is a framework to help succinctly form reflective answers. Many interviewers will be familiar with the STARR structure and will recognise its value.

- **S**ituation - describe the situation you were involved in
- **T**ask - explain the task you (or the doctor you were observing) had to complete
- **A**ction - describe the action undertaken
- **R**esult - explain what happened as a direct consequence of the actions taken
- **R**eflection - describe how this experience has impacted you, what have you learnt and try to give examples of actions you have taken as a result

Example

Situation	During my work experience, I had the opportunity to shadow a consultant gastroenterologist and observe their day-to-day work.
Task	While I was there one of the patients on the ward become critically unwell and I was able to observe the consultant breaking this bad news to the family.
Action	I noticed the doctor remained calm and allowed the relatives time to process the news and ask as many questions as needed, despite the doctor being very busy that day.
Result	As a result, the family felt secure and supported by the doctor. Even though a relative became angry at one point, the calmness of the doctor ensured that this did not escalate.
Reflection	This experience demonstrated the importance of empathy in healthcare and how the nature of how information is delivered can have large impacts on how it is received. I have tried to apply this to my own work in retail by giving customers space and time to process when mistakes happen.

Getting started

When you are conducting your work experience it is useful to keep a diary of your observations and review this prior to any interviews. Similarly, some students like to create a mind map of each placement to reflect on what they saw and learnt and how this could be applied to potential interview questions.

You should aim to have a set of well thought-out and reflected points developed from your work experience that you are prepared to mention in multiple interview scenarios.

Timing Tip

You will not have time to mention every interesting aspect of every work experience placement you have carried out. Be selective about what scenarios you discuss and make sure these are those that display the highest quality reflections. It is much easier to do this if you have prepared in advance.

The remainder of this section will discuss questions relating to the three most common work experience settings: GP, hospitals and surgery. Remember you do not need to have completed placements in all of these settings and a large variety of types work experience could be incorporated into your answers instead.

3.2 GP Work Experience

Conducting work experience in a GP practice is a great way of experiencing the NHS front line. GPs are usually the first contact when a patient becomes unwell meaning a huge variety of presentations walk through the door.

What can I expect on GP work experience?

No two work experience placements are the same and you are not expected to see a minimum number of consultations or complete a set list of activities. However, if you mention undertaking a GP-based work experience placement you could be asked about specific aspects of GP care as it is expected that you will have observed, or discussed, common activities that GPs perform during their daily work.

Take a look at your work experience diary and try to find examples where you observed to following aspects of GP care.

Same day or emergency appointments These for are patients who need to be seen urgently and are typically booked into a number of empty slots, kept aside for this specific purpose, with the "duty doctor". Sometimes other doctors may also book patients at the end of their clinics too - how do you think they manage this in terms of timing?

Pre-booked or routine appointments These are for patients with non-urgent problems who can wait days to weeks for an appointment slots. This could be used for medication reviews, following-up chronic diseases and delivering routine test results. Did you observe any differences in the types of conditions seen at these appointments?

Telephone consultations Telephone consultations are being utilised increasingly in both primary and secondary care settings. Can you think of any limitations or benefits of this? If you observed a telephone consultation, think about how the doctor adapted their communication style compared to a traditional face-to-face appointment.

Nurse appointments Sitting in on nurse clinics is a great way to understand the differences between the job roles of nurses and doctors. Think about any differences you observed - was this what you expected? You may find nurses carry out more traditionally "doctor jobs" than you initially expected! How did this influence your motivation to study medicine?

Reception work You may have been presented with the opportunity to sit with a GP receptionist. This provides an appreciation of the impact non-clinical staff can have on patient care. Can you think of any examples of good care or communication provided by one of the receptionists?

Practice questions

How do GP practices prioritise patients?

"As a GP's work is under time pressure, it is critical that patients who are more seriously unwell are given priority. When I undertook a work experience placement at a local GP practice, patients were initially booked for short telephone consultations. The GP used these telephone calls to assess the severity of symptoms and determine which patients needed to be seen in-person that day. In some

cases the GP was confident enough to diagnose over the phone, which had the benefit of saving the patient time to come into the surgery.

While the telephone triage system can save time, I recall a scenario where a patient became upset with the system as they felt that they had not been properly assessed due to not being physically examined. This made me consider the patient perspective and how a patient being triaged as non-urgent could be interpreted as receiving a lower standard of care. Some GP practices have opted to use alternative triaging systems for this, among other reasons."

Explanation This question is looking for candidates to have considered the important task of *triage*, which refers to the process of deciding which order patients should be seen in. The student is able to reflect on their work experience to describe the prioritisation process they observed, while also having an appreciation of positive and negative aspects of the system.

How long did each appointment last for? Did you feel this was an appropriate appointment length?

"Each GP appointment is typically just 10 minutes long as standard. I found that for some patients this was sufficient to explore their symptoms and recommend a management plan. However, for some patients with more complex, or multiple, issues the 10 minute time slot was restrictive to the amount of depth that could be explored.

For example, I can recall a particular patient who came to her appointment regarding a rash. The GP skilfully fully explored her symptoms and prescribed a treatment within the appointment slot, but just as the consultation was ending the patient admitted she was struggling with her mental health and wanted to discuss this too. This demonstrated difficult having such tight time limits can be, as time efficiency must be balanced with showing you care and have time for the patient without them feeling rushed."

Explanation GP appointment times are often difficult to stick to, but 10 minutes is standard across the UK. Patients frequently complain about being called later than their appointment time due to previous appointments over-running which can strain the doctor-patient relationship before the appointment has even began. This question is looking for a student to understand the strain of appointment length on GPs and to demonstrate some insight into the challenges this poses for doctors.

What is the role and importance of the GP receptionist?

"I was lucky enough to spend an afternoon with the reception team while on my work experience placement in a GP practice. I observed the GP receptionists booking appointments, dealing with patient requests and liaising with doctors and nurses when needed. Overall, my time with the reception staff demonstrated the importance of organisation within healthcare systems, as without the work performed by reception staff the whole system would cease to function."

Explanation By asking this question, an interviewer is making sure candidates have an understanding and appreciation for the critical work other members of the healthcare team perform to improve patient care, including the role of non-clinical staff.

What are the skills required by a GP?

"A GP needs to be knowledgeable and up-to-date in the management of conditions spanning every medical speciality. Additionally, many soft-skills are required for good clinical practice including, open mindedness, time efficiency and the ability to multi-task.

During my work experience I particularly noticed the need for a GP to possess strong communication skills. GPs see a wide variety of patients who have a range of communication needs. A GP needs to be in-tune with and be able to adapt to these varying needs within a short timeframe. For example, I recall the GP seeing an elderly patient for whom English was their second language and then in the next appointment, just 10 minutes later, they had to communicate with an anxious parent of an unwell toddler."

<u>Explanation</u> This question is an excellent opportunity to discuss observations you made during your GP work experience. There is a vast number of skills you could mention, but try to pick a handful to discuss in depth with support from scenarios in your work experience. An excellent answer would reflect on these experiences and provide examples where they also demonstrate the skill in question.

Practice MMI station

<u>Station brief</u> Do you think that non-emergency NHS care, such as GP services, should be provided 7 days a week?

Good answer A good answer will include:

- Balanced opinion with both pros and cons of a 7 day NHS discussed
- Points illustrated by examples - for example, can you think of a patient you met during work experience who would have benefited from services being available to them on the weekend?
- Thinking outside of the box and attempting to providing a solution

Points for and against providing 7 day GP care are given in the table below, but remember this is not exhaustive and you may have thought of valid points not mentioned here.

Pros	Cons
Improved patient care as full patient services available on weekends	Increased stress for doctors, leading to poorer morale and less efficiency which could result in more mistakes
Stops consultants from opting out as consultants can current decide to not perform non-emergency work at weekends, which can be detrimental to NHS	Less desire to be a doctor and reduced number of applications for jobs which involve more weekend hours
Increased doctor wages as a higher proportion of working hours will be "unsociable"	Discussion of wages as there may not be available funds to increase wages on weekends

Poor answer A poor will include:

- Biased opinions too heavily focused towards either positive or negative aspects
- Unable to use own experiences to help frame an opinion
- Many points listed, but only superficial depth of knowledge demonstrated
- Lack   of   understanding   of   current   out-of-hours   systems   in   the   NHS

3.3 Hospital Work Experience

Hospital work experience provides an opportunity to become familiar with the day-to-day running of a medical ward and gain an understanding of secondary care in the NHS.

What can I expect for hospital work experience?

There are an abundance of medical specialties and each hospital will have different departments available for students to conduct work experience. While your placement experiences will depend on the specialism you are placed in, the common ward-based activities listed below are a good starting point to begin forming your reflections.

Take a look at the notes you made during work experience and see which aspects of hospital care you could mention during an interview.

Ward rounds Ward rounds are a staple of medical inpatient care and involve a senior doctor, accompanied by other members of the team, reviewing each patient under their care. Consider how the team interacted during any ward rounds you observed. How were tasks delegated, and what role did each person play?

Clinics You may have had the opportunity to observe consultations in the outpatient department, meaning patients are seen that are not currently admitted to the hospital wards. If you have also conducted a GP placement, try and contrast the differences between the two different clinics you have seen.

Procedures Some medical specialties lend themselves towards conducting different types of procedures on the wards. Examples could include echocardiograms, bronchoscopy or line insertions. Did the procedural aspect of a doctor's job appeal to you? How could you demonstrate an aptitude for practical skills?

Investigations and their interpretation A key aspect of medicine is the ability to order and interpret test results. For example, during a typical shift a doctor may need to analyse X-rays, ECGs and blood results. Consider how the doctors you observed decided which tests each patient needed. What would the dangers of over- or under-investigating patients be?

Multidisciplinary meetings During these meetings a team of healthcare professionals, often crossing multiple specialties, will discuss selected cases to make decisions regarding a patients care. This provides an opportunity for input from several different disciplines, including allied healthcare professions. If you observed an MDT, think about examples of good or poor teamwork you noticed.

Practice questions

What did you notice about the skills doctors needed as they examined patients or took a patient's history?

"Hospital medicine requires a plethora of skills alongside clinical knowledge to be used by doctors. For example, even during a single morning on my work experience placement I noticed the doctor employ patience and empathy by listening and validating a patient's concerns, together with rapport building, practical   skills,   time   keeping   and   prioritisation   of   tasks.

A particular moment that stands out to me is the way a junior doctor dealt with an angry patient. The patient was frustrated at the length of time they had been waiting, however the doctor was able to de-escalate the situation by remaining calm and skillfully explaining the situation. This demonstrated to me how every patient encounter requires a complex skill set, as this single scenario involved empathy, active listening, resilience and honesty. "

Explanation The list of skills required by doctors is extensive - use this question as an opportunity to discuss any skill or quality that you can discuss in depth. Ensure your answer is backed up with direct observations from your work experience and includes discussion exploring why this skill is essential and how the student intends to develop it.

Doctors often take a holistic approach. What do we mean by this?

"A holistic approach encompasses considering all factors, be it physical, mental or social, in relation to health when assessing a patient. By doing this a doctor places value, not only to the physical disease process, but on the context in which this occurs.

I was able to observe examples of good holistic practice firsthand during my work experience in a hospital. I can recall a patient who was unfortunately diagnosed with a cancer during their stay on the ward. I was encouraged to see the doctor not only took time to explain the diagnosis and treatment, but also ensured to discuss the patient's mental wellbeing and impact on their life such as ability to care for children and taking time off work. I found it inspiring to see how appreciative the patient was, even during such a challenging time, and I look forward to practicing such holistic care when i become a doctor. "

Explanation This questions aims to explore a candidate's understanding of holistic care, and to identify any particularly good examples of patient care observed during work experience. The role of a doctor is increasingly moving beyond clinical activities and includes a greater consideration of social aspects in the biopsychosocial model of disease.

Can you think of some difficulties or challenges of being a doctor in a hospital?

"Even though medicine is an incredibly rewarding career, there are numerous challenges to the job too. I spent part of my work experience shadowing junior doctors on an acute medicine ward in my local hospital. I was struck by how busy their day was with long hours and a seemingly never-ending list of jobs and tasks. I also observed how some patients have unrealistic expectations, for example expecting to be seen very quickly. This made me reflect on how doctors may often receive complaints for situations out of their control. This being said, I was also able to observe the rewarding nature of the job and overall feel that the benefits outweigh the disadvantages making me excited to begin my career!"

Explanation All medical school applicants should have a **realistic** understanding of a career in medicine, including the drawbacks and challenges. It would be impossible to undertake a work experience placement and not notice some of the negative aspects to being a doctor. By asking this question, the interviewer is assessing a candidate's ability to be honest and checking they do not have idealised or unrealistic expectations for their career.

Tell me about your experiences observing a ward round.

"The ward round I attended was on a cardiac unit and was attended by numerous members of the team. The round was led by the consultant and supported by two junior doctors, a pharmacist and a nurse specialist. I found it inspiring to observe the good teamwork displayed. Every member of the team had a role to perform and worked together seamlessly. A notable moment occurred when

the consultant asked the junior doctor prescribed a drug, and the pharmacist noticed a prescribing error and tactfully corrected the doctor before it was administered. To me, this illustrates the complimentary value of other health professionals to a doctor's work."

<u>Explanation</u> There are many valuable observations that could be made from a simple ward round. This answer highlights the teamwork demonstrated between different healthcare professionals, but equally the candidate could have mentioned empathy, communication or organisation.

3.4 Surgical Work Experience

A surgeon is type of doctor who specialises in treating patients by performing operations. There are many subspecialties within surgery from neurosurgery to orthopaedics and even fetal surgery! The collaboration between surgeons, hospital physicians and GPs is crucial to their work and the care of the patient, therefore even if you have little intention of pursuing surgery as a career, all doctors should be aware of the work they do.

What can I expect on surgical work experience?

Surgery is a diverse field, and with the introduction of modern technology operations can be more varied than ever before. The majority of candidates will not have had surgical work experience, therefore do not worry if you have not experienced the operating theatre environment. For those students who are lucky enough to have had a surgical placement you could reflect on or mention any of the following aspects of surgical care.

Observing operations Witnessing operations is probably the aspect of surgical that students look forward to the most. It is something quite unlike any other area of medicine, and is truly a fortunate opportunity. Operations can either performed as an emergency or elective, meaning they have been planned in advance.

Common pitfall

Remember that work experience is not about what you have done, but rather what you learnt and took away from the experience. Interviewers will not be fooled by candidates who simply list complex procedures they have witnessed in a bid to be impressive. Instead, reflect on the experience including simple interactions between colleagues.

Members of the surgical team The surgical team is far wider than just the surgeons who perform the operation. You will come across operating department practitioners, theatre nurses, radiographers, surgical assistants among others. Try and talk to as many different staff members as possible and understand what their role is and how it impacts the patient.

Clinics Not all surgical care occurs in the operating theatre. Just as in medical specialties, there will be surgical ward rounds and clinics. Patients will often attend clinic to be investigated for diagnoses, to consent for operations and postoperatively for follow-up care. How may surgical clinics differ from those of a GP, for example?

Preoperative and anaesthetic care The surgeon is not the only doctor present for operations! An anaesthetist is a doctor who specialises on putting patients to sleep for operations and managing their pain. Try to talk to an anaesthetist during your placement and consider what different skills this role may required compared to a surgeon.

Practice questions

What is the role of the medical team in a patient's care after an operation?

"My work experience taught me that the patient journey is far from over once the operation is finished. In many aspects, the weeks following an operation and the recovery process is just as

important as the procedure itself. The medical team is crucial to ensuring the recovery period is as optimal as possible, maximising the chance of a good outcome for the patient.

I spent a week shadowing the team on an inpatient orthopaedic unit. After orthopaedic surgery the patients were relatively immobile and relied on the input on physiotherapists to help restore joint function and occupational therapists to provide support returning to everyday activities. The doctors were also crucial outside of the operating theatre, from the junior doctors who optimised pain relief and checked for complications, to the surgical team who follow-up patients up long term."

Explanation The key aspect of this question is to recognise that the team caring for a patient is not just made up of doctors. If you have been on a ward you will have noticed the vast number of professionals involved in each patients care - this question is asking you to reflect on the different roles you have come across.

What skills does a surgeon have?

"Like all doctors surgeons are required to be knowledgeable, work in a team and have good communication skills. In addition, due to the practical nature of their job, a surgeon must have incredible manual dexterity skills. During my work experience I was amazed by how small some of the anatomical structures operated on were, which reinforced the importance of precision to a surgeon's work.

I was given the opportunity to observe a cesarean section during my work experience. Unfortunately, there were complications as the patient began to bleed heavily. This scenario, while initially startling to me, demonstrated how a surgeon's ability to maintain composure in difficult situations is critical. I noticed how the surgeons demeanor often sets the tone of the room, which was particularly key in this case as the patient was awake."

Explanation Different types of doctors draw on different skill sets and this question is asking candidate's to reflect on their observations of surgeons to discuss the skills particularly relevant to their job. An excellent candidate would suggest ways in which they have, or plan to, develop these same skills.

Have you read an article or interesting news topic relating to surgery?

"I have recently read an article in a national newspaper regarding the current waiting times for elective operations, with tens of thousands of patients having waited over two years. I found this article interesting as it demonstrates one of the long term impacts COVID-19 will have on the NHS and doesn't have a clear solution. I also saw this firsthand during work experience, where the patients I met having joint replacements had been waiting for the operation since before the pandemic, often having had multiple procedures canceled in the preceding years."

Explanation By showing evidence of further reading around topics relevant to work experience, the candidate is showing they are genuinely interested in medicine and have the drive to learn more. Similarly a medical student may be expected to use their evenings to read up on conditions they have seen on placement that day. If you are asked a question like this, expect to be asked follow-up questions about your opinions - consequently never pretend to have read something you have not!

3.5 Practice Questions: Work Experience

1. What did you learn from your work experience?
2. Can you tell me about a memorable situation you observed, and what you learned from it?
3. What important qualities did you notice from doctors during your work experience?
4. Why do you think we want our applicants to do work experience?
5. How did your work experience change your view of the NHS or medicine in general?
6. After an operation, what is the role of the medical team in the patient's care?
7. Apart from the operating theatre, did you shadow the surgeons in another setting such as a clinic?
8. What are the current issues in the NHS surrounding surgeries? Did you observe any of these?
9. What are the challenges of being a surgeon?
10. What do you feel about the telephone triage system used in many General Practices?
11.
12. What are the challenges of being a GP?
13. Do you think GPs should have telephone consultations as an option for patients?
14. Do you feel that the public's perception of a GP is misrepresentative?
15. What did you notice about the skills doctors needed when they were carrying out a patient history?
16. What did you notice about the doctors you were shadowing in their approach to patients?
17. What were the roles of different members of the multidisciplinary team during a ward round?
18. What challenges did you observe the doctor face whilst on work experience? How did they overcome them?
19. What is something you observed a doctor do during work experience that you would have done differently?
20. What was the most enjoyable part of your work experience?
21. Describe a time that you observed a doctor delivering good communication skills.
22. What is something you saw a doctor do that you feel could be improved?
23. Who is the most important member of a multidisciplinary health care team?
24. Is there anything about how hospitals are run that you would change?
25. What did you find most surprising whilst doing your work experience?
26. What does the term "holistic care" mean to you?
27. What did the doctors do during your work experience that impressed you the most?
28. What did you hope to gain from your work experience?
29. Who inspired you the most during your work experience?
30. Was your experience of work experience placements what you expected?

CHAPTER 4

IV Personal Qualities & Skills

4.1 Introduction

Questions concerning a candidate's personal qualities and skills are very common in medical school interviews. As we discussed in the introduction to this book, the GMC's "*Duties of a Doctor*" provides a guidance on the kind of skills expected of anyone entering medicine. However, interviewers are not only expecting students to identify the skills required of a doctor. Candidates are also expected to demonstrate how they have begun developing these skills themselves.

It is important to prepare in advance and reflect on your own personality traits in the context of medicine. This type of question can take on many different forms so it is useful to use a framework that you can refer to when constructing an answer.

Medic Mind's framework for discussing skills and personal qualities

Students often struggle to construct answers discussing their personal qualities or skills that are effective and succinct. We have evolved a 5-step method of approaching these questions. Our method encourages you to prepare discussion points for several skills, without running the risk of your answers sounding rehearsed or formulaic. It can also be applied to several types of questions on personal qualities and skills, so you will be well prepared for any question that you are presented with.

Step 1: Pick 3 extracurricular activities

Consider all the extracurricular activities you have taken part in over the past few years. This could include volunteering, part-time work, hobbies, school societies and clubs among many others. The first step is to select three of these activities that could link to medicine and showcase your achievements in the best possible light. Try to choose activities that involve different personal qualities and skills, so that each example you discuss in your answer is unique.

Example

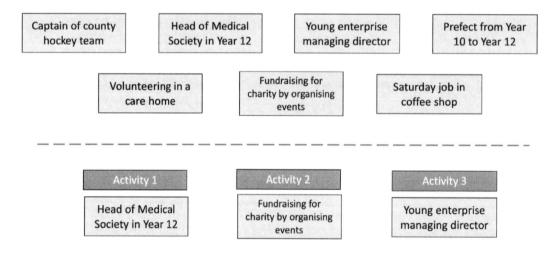

Step 2: Pick 5 skills or qualities

With the selected extracurricular activities in mind, consider all the skills and qualities you have shown and developed when undertaking these activities. Select five of these skills that you are most confident in discussing   and   illustrate   your   best   qualities.

Example

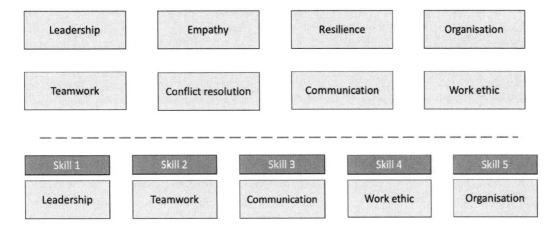

Step 3: Link achievements to skills

Review the extracurricular activities selected in Step 1 and assign the relevant skills that are demonstrated by each particular undertaking. Link together the skills and activities to form a list.

Example

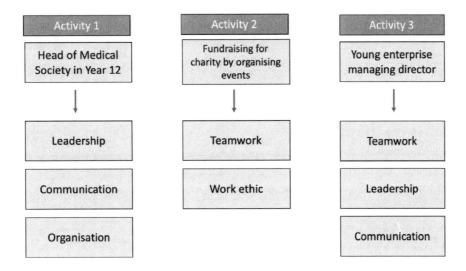

Step 4: Pick one activity per skill

The next step is to narrow down the list, so that each skill is assigned to just one activity. The objective of this step is to ensure you have a different example for each of you best qualities and skills. This will ensure that you do not repeat examples when answering this type of question in the interview.

Example

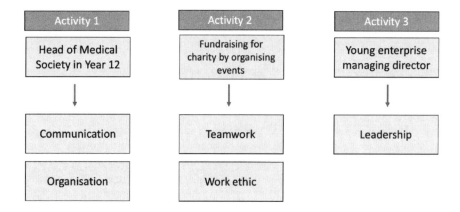

Step 5: Link back to medicine

Finally, link each skill back to medicine and explain how it would be relevant to a doctor. Think about the day-to-day responsibilities of a doctor, and the types of challenges a doctor might face. You could refer to articles or documentaries that provide an insight into the profession or situations that you have witnessed during your own work experience in a GP or hospital.

Then, try to link a relevant scenario or challenge to each of the personal qualities and skills in your list. This will ensure that the personal qualities, skills and examples you are discussing are sufficiently relevant to the field of medicine. It will also allow you to demonstrate a strong understanding of what the field of medicine involves and requires

Example

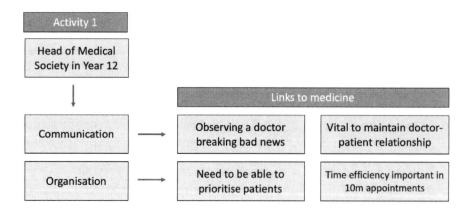

Sample responses

What is your greatest strength?

"I believe that I work well as a leader, so leadership is one of my strongest skills. As managing director of my young enterprise company, Derive, I developed the skills of delegation and management. I aim to be approachable to my team members, and work hard to lead by example. This will serve me well as a doctor, a career in which I may manage teams in lots of settings."

<u>Feedback</u> By using the Medic Mind framework this student has prepared for this question prior to the interview. The candidate is able to select a strong skill of their choice, describe a scenario that

demonstrates and explain how this will be useful in their future career. The structure ensures all key elements are delivered succinctly.

Give three adjectives that best describe you.

"The first adjective I would use to describe myself is organised. Alongside studying for my A-Level exams, I have taken on multiple additional responsibilities such as Head of the Medical Society over the past year. This required substantial organisation, to ensure smooth running of all society activities, alongside meeting academic deadlines and maintaining grades. Developing strong organisation skills is important for a career as a doctor where prioritisation of tasks and patients is key. I would also describe myself using the adjectives leader and empathetic."

Feedback This question invites candidates to discuss three skills of their choice. You may not have time to fully explore each skill and link it back to medicine. This answer opts to discuss organisation in full, and simply mentions leadership and empathy without discussing any achievements or links to medicine. It is important to be flexible with your approach in the context of strict time limits found in MMI stations.

4.2 Qualities of a Doctor

A career in medicine requires a host of specialised skills knowledge. However, a successful doctor will also possess many "soft" skills in addition to their scientific knowledge. A "soft" skill is one that often forms part of a person's personality and represents the qualities required to form a strong doctor-patient relationship and are crucial to provide excellent care. They are non-technical skills that relate to the way you work, such as interactions with colleagues and managing a heavy workload. Medical school applicants should expect for certain elements of their personality to be assessed during an interview, as these qualities affect interactions with everyone from patients, to colleagues, to a patient's relatives.

Important qualities of a doctor

As discussed in the introduction to this book, the GMC publishes *'Duties of a Doctor'* which details the expectations of all registered doctors. This document provides a framework for the types of "soft" skills expected of doctors, and consequently of medical students and applicants too.

The number of skills required in a doctor is far-reaching, but common examples include:

- Teamwork
- Leadership
- Communication
- Organisation
- Empathy
- Compassion
- Scientific knowledge
- Manual dexterity
- Calmness

Applicants to medical school should expect to be asked questions about skills more generally, such as *"What is the most important skill for a doctor?"*, which requires reflection and recognition of the multiple qualities essential to practice medicine. Interviewers may also ask about specific skills, for example *"Why is good communication important?"*, and are looking for understanding of the importance of that specific skill and reflections on a candidate's own abilities within that domain.

Expert's Advice

When asking about skills and personality, an interviewer may not ask about work experience directly. However these questions are an excellent opportunity to incorporate reflections of good practice you have observed. Simply stating that teamwork is important will not score highly - instead, a good candidate will explain the importance of teamwork and contribute their own experiences to strengthen their answer.

Sample responses

What   is   more   important   as   a   doctor   -   being   intelligent   or   having   empathy?

"Intelligence is a key attribute for a good doctor. Practicing medicine requires a deep understanding of the scientific processes occurring inside the body as well as knowledge of pathophysiology, anatomy and pharmacology. In addition, a career in medicine requires constant learning as new advances are made and consequently the ability to adapt and carry out lifelong study is important.

However, medicine also requires a high level of social intelligence, of which empathy is a key part. Overall I would say that while both intelligence and empathy are vital skills for any doctor, in some regards intelligence could be viewed as more important. Medicine is a holistic art, and communicating with patients requires a comforting and reassuring manner - without this a patient may struggle to relate and open up. My reasoning is that a doctor who is extremely empathetic but without the required scientific knowledge, will not be able to reach the correct diagnoses or select an appropriate treatment required to help that patient."

<u>Feedback</u> This is a good answer. The candidate explains the importance of both qualities, giving a balanced answer. The answer could additionally be strengthened by using examples from work experience or extracurricular activities that demonstrate the importance of either scientific knowledge or empathy in medicine. A strong element of this answer is a final conclusion that sums up their view and makes a decision without sitting on the fence.

Common Pitfall

It is important to recognise that there is often no wrong answer to questions like this. An equally good candidate may have been able to justify empathy as the final answer. Remember it is not the final answer that will score you marks - it is how you reason and reach your conclusions.

> If you were on the admissions board at this medical school, what skills or qualities would look for in applicants?

Example 1 *"There are many qualities to look for in future doctors. There are some skills that you cannot learn so I would focus on identifying those innate caring skills. For example, communication skills, and the ability to adapt communication style between different groups. This requires a candidate to be able to recognise the communication needs of different groups. Unlike the core sciences, this is not something that can be taught in a lecture hall but is equally important for patient care."*

<u>Feedback</u> This is a poor answer. The candidate is only able to identify a single quality and does not reflect on their own experiences. They also suggest that "soft" skills, such as communication, cannot be taught. This is a dangerous statement - you might end up being interviewed by the lead communication skills lecturer so be very careful when making broad or generalised statements like this.

Example 2 *"The admissions board is looking to select candidates that demonstrate the potential to develop into excellent doctors including academic potential and the "soft" skills required for a career in medicine. Examples of the qualities I would be looking for include empathy, strong communication skills, resilience and compassion. In addition, an important skill to assess is teamwork as I believe it to be central to the modern healthcare system.*

During my work experience placement in a GP surgery, I unfortunately witnessed an example of poor communication. A patient attended the surgery for a nurse appointment. The nurse needed advice and clarification from the GP about the problem and sent them a virtual message. Unfortunately, key information was missed from the message and the GP provided incorrect advice. Subsequently the patient returned to the GP a week later after attending A&E due to complications of the initial problem. This illustrated to me the importance of strong teamwork skills as, in this case, the failure of multi-disciplinary team members to work well together results in a poor outcome for the patient."

Feedback This is a good answer. The candidate is able to identify suitable qualities for a medical student. Crucially, this answer explores one of these qualities in more depth by reflecting on a work experience scenario. With this question, be prepared for follow-up questions exploring your own abilities in whichever skills you have mentioned.

Practice MMI station

Station brief What attributes do you have that will make you a good doctor?

Good answer A good answer may include:

- Identification of multiple key qualities essential for doctors
- Acknowledgment that both "hard" and "soft" skills are important
- Reflection on work experience, giving an example of a situation where key skills were demonstrated by the professionals at work
- Demonstration of key skills being developed by the candidate through extracurricular activities

Poor answer A poor answer may include:

- Overemphasis on academic attributes and knowledge - remember that the purpose of medical school is to teach you the medical knowledge needed to become a doctor! While academic aptitude is important, in-depth medical knowledge is not required of an applicant.
- Superficial descriptions rather than deep reflection on own abilities and skills.

4.3 Teamwork

Being a strong team player is vital as a doctor. The healthcare sector requires individuals in different roles to work together in the patient's best interests. The multidisciplinary team will include other healthcare professionals, such as nurses and physiotherapists, but also doctors of varying specialties and seniority. Questions assessing teamwork ability, both in a leadership and team-player capacity, are among some of the most common medical school interview questions.

Common pitfall

Remember to put the Medic Mind framework into practice and incorporate the skill (teamwork) to an extracurricular activity you have undertaken, and finally explain how this is relevant to the medical profession.

Sample responses

What are some features of a good team player?

"A good team player will contribute to the overall success of the team in multiple different ways. A team player will not only recognise their own strengths but will recognise the key skills and strengths of others and support them to contribute their strong points. A team player needs to have good communication skills and be able to take direction from others. An example that illustrates this to me is my experience on the committee of the Medical Society in my school. We had a task to organise a fundraising event. A committee member was particularly experienced in fundraising, however the president of the society failed to appreciate this and attempted to organise the event by themselves. By not appreciating the significant experience of a team member, the president made multiple mistakes, wasted time and was less efficient overall. "

Feedback This is a good answer. The response gives a number of features of a good team player and uses an example to illustrate what a bad team player looks like. An excellent candidate would push this answer even further and describe features of their own personality that make them a good team player with ideas of how they plan to develop these skills.

Why is teamwork important?

Example 1 *"Teamwork is important as it allows the different strengths of each individual team member to combine. This means activities can be completed more efficiently based on each team members strengths. When I was on the Medical Society committee at school, my personal strengths were in design and marketing and consequently my role focused on designing posters and managing social media. Whereas other members of the team focused on accounts and finances, or liaising with staff members as this was their strengths."*

Feedback This is a weak answer. The candidate gives a good reason for the importance of teamwork, and is able to evidence this with personal experience. However this answer falls short as the student does not link or reflect on the way in which teamwork is applicable to medicine or a career as a doctor. The response would be significantly strengthened by suggesting ways in which the student will use their teamwork skills and strengths during medical school and beyond.

Example 2 *"Teamwork is important in many areas of life, but it is particularly important in a healthcare setting. In order to be successful, healthcare workers must act as a team to utilise the different skills each member contributes. It is important to understand that, even as a senior doctor, no single person will know everything about every possible illness. By working as a team, you are able to bounce off other people's strengths and skills to support each other to reach the best possible outcome for the patient.*

I saw a good example of this during my work experience on an orthopaedic ward. I noticed how each member of the team had a particular area of the patient's care that they focused on and very knowledgeable about. For example, the surgeon who performed the operations, but it was the physiotherapists who took a central role and were more knowledgeable in after-care and rehab as this area. This made me reflect on how important it is to recognise the boundaries of your own knowledge and be able to consult other team members in the future."

<u>Feedback</u> This is a good answer. The student shows they recognise some of the benefits of working in a team. They evidence this with observation from work experience and attempt to apply the lessons learnt to their future practice. This answer explains the importance of recognising your own limitations, which is a quality specifically listed by the GMC in *'Duties of a Doctor'*.

Practice MMI station

<u>Station brief</u> During your time at medical school you will have to work in small groups, both in tutorials and on hospital wards in later years.

Why do you think we incorporated a large amount of teamwork into our curriculum?

Good answer A good answer may include:

- Understanding of the role teams play within healthcare and the contribution of the multidisciplinary team. For example, during a surgical procedure there may be multiple surgeons, anaesthetists, nurses and specialised practitioners.
- Knowledge of the curriculum and how teamwork is incorporated at that medical school. The candidate should draw parallels with the group work during medical school and the expectations of a doctor to be a team player.
- Evidence of good teamwork carried out by the applicant, either as a team member or a leader.
- Suggestions for how the candidates skills may fit into teamwork during medical school.

Poor answer A poor answer may include:

- Focus on leadership. The days of doctors giving orders to other healthcare workers are gone. Modern medicine requires doctors to be equally talented team members and leaders depending on the situation.
- Not answering the question fully with reference to the use of teamwork in the curriculum. Some candidates may interpret this question to be asking the merits of teamwork in general and despite giving an excellent explanation, will fail to score points as they do not answer the specific question.

4.4 Leadership

A doctor will often take on a leadership role within the healthcare team. While other healthcare professionals contribute valuable skills, a doctor is typically the ultimate decision maker in a patient's care. A medical school interview will assess your leadership potential by asking your perception of the qualities of a great leader, and by also asking you to draw on previous experiences of acting as a leader.

Common pitfall

Leadership and teamwork questions are often asked together, perhaps even in the same MMI station. It is important to differentiate between the two as a strong doctor will act as both a leader and team member depending on the scenario.

If you have spent time in an operating theatre during work experience you will have observed firsthand how a surgeon takes control and leads the team during surgery. The surgical environment is a great example of both teamwork and leadership. Within the surgical team every member has a clearly defined and important role which is vital for success of the operation. However, it is the surgeon who directs the progress of the procedure and draws on the expertise of other team members when needed.

Sample responses

What are some features of a good leader?

"A leader needs to be many things. They need to be motivational, organised and able to delegate appropriately. However in my opinion the best leaders are those who foster an environment that allows team members to feel comfortable to voice opinions and raise concerns. By doing so, the leader invites criticism in a safe environment so that conflicts or problems within any particular group or project can be addressed quickly.

An example of great leadership I have observed is the coach of my netball team. She is firm in her expectations yet when issues have arisen, such as episodes of bullying, she listened non-judgmentally to team members which enabled other issues to come to light. I have tried to mimic this in my own leadership roles. For example, last year I was elected Head Girl at my school and made the effort during speeches let the other students know that I was available to talk to them if they were facing difficulties. I hope to carry forward that approachability and ability to listen in future leadership scenarios as a doctor."

<u>Feedback</u> This is an excellent answer. The student gives a handful of qualities seen in good leaders, but expands on one particular element (approachability) in detail. This answer shows reflection on a good leader from an extracurricular activity, but then demonstrates how the candidate has put what they have learnt into action in their own life.

Do you prefer working alone or in a team?

"Teamwork and independent working both come with their benefits and challenges. Through working as a group, you can collaborate and draw upon the individual strengths of each team member to work more efficiently. Teams also help you avoid errors and allows you to get a second

opinion. For example, in a healthcare team a doctor is able to draw upon the knowledge of pharmacists who may identify prescribing errors or suggest a more effective treatment.

Working alone also has some advantages such as a greater degree of independence and ability to direct your work. While my personal preference would be to work in a team, I am also comfortable working independently and understand that a doctor must be able to do both in different settings. I know teamwork takes a central role in learning at this medical school, through the problem-based learning approach. The opportunity to work in a group for a significant part of my studies is something that attracted me to apply here."

<u>Feedback</u> This is a good answer. The student is able to appreciate the benefits of both independent and group work, but is able to make a choice between the two and justify this. The inclusion of a healthcare-related examples shows a degree of reflection on how teamwork fits into the work of a doctor.

Expert's Advice

Remember that a question asking you to pick between two options often has no right or wrong answer. An interviewer is looking for a balanced answer and a reasonable justification for the option you decide. Try not to get caught up in which option to choose in the conclusion to your answer, instead focus on how to explore the reasoning behind that choice.

Practice MMI station

<u>Station brief</u> You are working on a group project as part of the coursework during your degree. Team members are expected to contribute equally to the task.

Initially the project was going well but now one particular member of the group, Layla, has stopped attending group meetings and is not meeting deadlines relevant to her parts. This has gone on for several weeks and is negatively impacting on your progress as a group.

As the group leader, how would you approach this situation?

Good answer A good answer may include:

- Awareness of some of the reasons a student may withdraw from a group task such as illness, stress and burnout.
- Approaching Layla with compassion and empathy. A good leader is non-judgemental and sensitive to group members experiencing difficulties
- Escalating to staff only if unable to resolve the issue within the group, or if Layla reveals a serious reason underlying her absence and requires external help.
- Provides pragmatic solutions or strategies to support Layla.

Poor answer A poor answer may include:

- Reporting or consulting to staff members directly. As a leader you should try and resolve the problem yourself first, especially as it is not too serious.
- Being overly confrontational. Empathy is an important quality and you should consider why Layla has changed her behaviour recently.
- Generates friction within the group by involving other group members and drawing attention to Layla's   lack   of   contribution.

4.5 Empathy

Medicine is often regarded as being both an art and a science - your biomedical knowledge of the workings of the body is applied in a holistic approach taking into account the social and emotional needs of that individual patient. Empathy has become something of a buzzword for medical school interviews and will certainly be assessed in some shape or form. However, ensure you fully understand the meaning of empathy and the important role it plays in all healthcare settings.

Empathy and sympathy

The distinction between empathy and sympathy is a common topic in medical school interviews. These two concepts are very similar but it is important to feel confident clearly explaining the differences.

Common Pitfall

Some candidates fall into the trap of using empathy and sympathy interchangeably. While the difference between the two terms can appear subtle at first, there is a key distinction to understand. Both terms relate to ways of handling emotions in difficult situations, but empathy is a much deeper response.

Both empathy and sympathy are useful in different situations. Empathy refers to the ability to share the feelings of another. In other words, empathy is putting yourself in another person's shoes to experience their emotions and understanding their point of view. On the other hand, sympathy describes the feeling of pity or sorrow for another person. In medicine sympathy can come across as patronising or isolation, regardless of how well-meaning, so is better avoided. Empathy promotes a connection between patient and doctor, whereas sympathy fuels disconnection.

Consider the situation where a patient is in hospital and experiencing severe pain. The phrase *"I am sorry this is happening to you"* suggests that the speaker does not share the patient's experience of pain. This lends to the tendency to "talk down" and creates a division between the person who is suffering and the person who is not. Whereas the alternative phrase *"I can see that things must be very hard for you right now"* shows empathy as the speaker has imagined what it is like to be the patient, and validated their experience. They are understanding of the problem and, even though the pain is not physically shared, they are accepting without making the problem about themselves.

Sample responses

What does the word empathy mean to you?

"Empathy describes the experience of putting yourself in someone elses's shoes and understanding their point of view. Without empathy a doctor would not understand the experiences of our patients and may ignore or be ignorant to factors important to their care. By showing empathy, a patient is more likely to feel an emotional connection to their doctor and this may prompt them to disclose sensitive information, or follow the doctors advice.

During my GP work experience I can remember a particular moment where the doctor displayed immense empathy. A mother came in for a health check after giving birth and disclosed she did not plan on vaccinating her child. Instead of being paternalistic or disapproving, the doctor was non-judgemental and asked the patient to share her concerns. Even though the doctor did not personally share the views of the patient, she validated her concerns by empathising that any new mother would be concerned about the risks of a medical intervention. By doing this, the doctor was able to gently challenge the mother without causing a confrontation. "

<u>Feedback</u> As with all questions about personal qualities, make sure to link the answer back to medicine and why it is relevant for a career as a doctor. This answer could have been strengthened by deeper reflection by exploring how the student plans to use empathy in their future studies or career.

Are you an empathetic person?

"Empathy is a key skill for doctors, and all members of the healthcare team. As a doctor it is important to show empathy to your patients to strengthen the doctor-patient relationship. I believe myself to be an empathetic person. For example, over the past year I have been volunteering in a care home on the weekends. My role involves helping out with activities and facilitating socialisation between the residents.

During one session, a resident began to tell me about the death of her husband and became visibly upset. I made a cup of tea for us both and sat down in a quiet area with her. I displayed empathy by acknowledging her sorrow and encouraging her to share her memories if she felt comfortable. It was heartening for me at the end of the day when she expressed her gratitude for my kindness. "

<u>Feedback</u> This answer gives a good answer of a time where the candidate demonstrated empathy. The first paragraph links the skill to medicine and shows an understanding of why empathy is important within healthcare.

Common Pitfall

This question focuses on you and is asking for you to share your own experience of empathy. Some candidates fail to recognise this and instead may reflect on a time they witnessed empathy during their work experience. This does not show the interviewer how they themselves are empathetic and consequently will not score highly. If a question asks about you specifically, make sure you use examples where you have directly contributed.

Practice MMI stations

<u>Station brief</u> This station will focus on exploring your personal qualities and how these make you suitable to become a doctor.

As a doctor you will have to break bad news and deal with situations where things go wrong. How will you cope with this emotionally?

Good answer A good answer may:

• Understand the importance of relating to a patient when breaking bad news. We need to show empathy to avoid being overly cold or clinical.

- A good candidate will also avoid being overly emotional. There is a balance between being too corporate and too sentimental. Healthcare professionals need to keep an emotional distance in order to think properly and behave appropriately.
- Reference any work experience or volunteering. Reflection on observations of difficult situations or describing how a candidate has developed their own communication skills would strengthen an answer.

Poor answer A poor answer may:

- Admit that this is an area where the candidate would struggle. A surprising number of candidates respond to this question by saying they are emotional and will find breaking bad news too challenging.
- Being apathetic. Some candidates say they would approach difficult situations by being fully unemotional and detached, treating the patient as a scientific case.

Station brief You are a third year medical student studying for your exams. Your friend, Simon, asks to meet with you after a particularly long and stressful day on placement. He tells you he cannot cope with life at medical school and wishes to drop out to go traveling instead. He is asking for your advice on how to communicate this decision to his parents.

Notes for actor (Simon) You are feeling incredibly anxious for the upcoming third year exams. You have not started revision and can not find the motivation to do so. Your parents have always wanted you to become a doctor and the weight of their expectations plays on your mind a lot. Your main worry is failing your exams and disappointing your parents in this way.

Good answer A good answer will:

- Use active listening skills to fully explore Simon's point of view and the factors leading up to his decision to leave medical school.
- Use empathetic phrases to encourage Simon to open up, for example *"I can see that you're struggling at the moment"* or *"This must be a very difficult situation"*.

Poor answer A poor answer will include:

- Judgmental views or immediately persuading Simon to stay. Without knowing Simon's background we cannot know if dropping out of medical school is the right thing for him to do. Although studying medicine may be the correct career path for the candidate, we cannot assume this is true for Simon too.
- Quick attempts to fix the problem without understanding fully Simon's point of view. Often being empathetic is less about solving the issue, but listening and encouraging the other person to find their own solutions.
- Sympathetic phrases rather than empathetic. Try to avoid inserting your own views or experiences into your responses. This conversation should be about Simon and his experience.

4.6 Organisation

During medical school and throughout a career in medicine, it is vital to remain organised and on top of the vast amount of work given. If you have spent time in a GP practice during work experience you will have observed the multitude of different tasks the GP is required to perform in short 10 minute appointment slots. Even while at medical school, students need to be able to balance the demands of studying alongside attending placements, maintaining a social life and taking part in hobbies.

Prioritisation and learning to making decisions depending on the urgency of different tasks is crucial to efficient working. A patient with a life threatening condition needs to be seen sooner than a patient with a minor ailment. These prioritisation skills, or 'triaging' can be applied to studying too. For example, a student who focuses revising for an imminent rather than a piece of coursework that is not due until the following month is more likely to be successful. In this chapter we will discuss various organisation skills and questions regarding a student's ability to manage their time.

Time management strategies

It is useful to have a number of time management strategies prepared to use in relevant questions. These could be examples of organisation skills you already employ to manage your school work, or plans to avoid burnout. You do not need to mention every possible organisation skill or strategy. Incorporate the methods that are relevant to you and for which you would genuinely use in your further studies.

Keeping a diary One of the most simple but effective time management strategies is using a diary or planner. This allows you to keep track of deadlines and other important events in your schedule. You could even use a digital calendar or note-taking app for the same purpose.

Prioritisation of tasks Being able to your focus attention on the tasks that are most important is a critical skill to learn. The ability to identify the most urgent areas of work is a skill that should not be underestimated. Strategies enabling prioritisation include constructing a prioritisation matrix or delegating less important tasks.

De-stress A medical career is often stressful and it is important to have strategies in place to avoid burnout. Medical schools are keen to see students recognising their own limitations and understanding the importance of a life outside of medicine. Your de-stress techniques do not have to be sophisticated and may be as simple as doing exercise or spending time with loved ones.

Making a list of tasks Constructing a to-do list is the fundamental basis of most organisation techniques. If you spent time on a hospital ward during work experience you may have noticed junior doctors constructing a 'jobs list' during the morning ward round. Writing a to-do list also facilitates prioritisation and planning ahead. For example, you may have lists for immediate tasks to be completed today as well as lists for the near and distant future.

Planning ahead Having an idea of upcoming tasks and events will allow you to plan accordingly. Medicine is a broad subject and during your time at medical school you are expected to learn a enormous amount of content. Leaving an entire module's worth of content to revise last minute is not an efficient strategy. Rather, planning ahead and ensuring you have sufficient time to fully cover the content is more favourable. Examples   of   this   strategy   that   you   could   mention   include constructing a revision timetable and allocating tasks to certain be completed in specific time frames.

Balancing time While it is helpful to plan ahead, remember to be flexible and allow for adjustments to you schedule too. The life of a doctor is unpredictable and sometimes you will need to change plans with very short notice. By incorporating a degree of flexibility into your organisation plans, a candidate demonstrates a realistic expectation of their career to the interviewers.

Common Pitfall

When discussing organisation during a medical school interview, always give a solution as part of your answer. Instead of simply saying you will balance your time, instead use examples of the methods you plan to employ to do so.

Sample responses

Tell me about a non-academic project in which you were involved.

"Over the past year I have held the position of Fundraising Lead for my sixth form. This role required me to organise all the fundraising activities in our school to support our chosen charities. The role was busy and involved managing a team of six students of varying ages as well as liasing with staff members and various charitable departments. This required a great deal of organisation to manage alongside revising for my A-Levels. For example, when arranging a particular event I realised that it would clash with some of my exams. To manage this I constructed a to-do list and prioritised the most important tasks that could be completed in advance. This allowed me to optimise the use of my time, while also leaving time to revise. Time management is an important skill for studying at medical school, as well as a career in medicine, and I hope to apply the skills I learned as Fundraising Lead to my future studies."

Feedback This question is not specifically asking about organisation or time management skills, but is a good opportunity to demonstrate them. The candidate could have equally chosen to use this question to demonstrate empathy, leadership or other key skills.

How do you plan to stay organised during medical school?

"To manage my time I ensure that I make lists to plan tasks, I prioritise in order of urgency for tasks, I use contingencies to account for tasks taking long and I take plenty of time to relax to destress. I also keep an up-to-date calendar."

Feedback This candidate has given some good strategies for remaining organised during medical school. However the answer fails to provide any evidence of further insight or explanation, and instead simply provides a list. Ensure that every point, or strategy, you mention in an answer is fully expanded. It is far better to take one or two points and fully explore them, than to simply list a larger number of points.

"Organising myself is something I'm used to from school. This year, I had to manage and organise my time effectively to ensure that I could participate in my charity fundraising team alongside my school work. To do this, I allocated set times to do my school work, and also made lists to ensure that I was aware of what had to be done. Of course, I also left time to relax, ensuring that when I did work I do so efficiently."

<u>Feedback</u> This is a stronger answer. The student uses examples from their charity work to illustrate clear examples using their chosen strategies in action. The final sentence mentions the importance of relaxing and leaving time to de-stress. This is a good way to finish the answer is it communicates to the interviewer that this candidate understands the importance of recreation and is unlikely to overwork themselves.

Practice MMI station

<u>Station brief</u> Medicine involves a great deal of independent study. How will you manage it?

Good answer A good answer may include:

- Understanding of the different activities a medical student undertakes in independent study e.g. clinical placements, preparing for PBL sessions and lectures.
- Reflection on own limitations and appropriate strategies to remain organised given the workload of a medical degree.
- Examples of time management for independent projects from previous projects or studies.
- Highlighting the importance of downtime to 'recharge' in order to remain efficient and avoid burnout.

Poor answer A poor answer may include:

- Dismissal or attempts to minimise the demands of a medical degree on students.
- Providing a list of organisation strategies without applying this to a medical context or explanation of how these would help the student.
- Admitting that organisation is a personal struggle and that it will be hard to manage independent studying alongside the demands of a medical degree.

4.7 Strengths and Weakness

In previous chapters we have discussed the approach to questions addressing specific skills such as teamwork, leadership and empathy. However, some questions are broader and ask candidates to self-identify areas of strength or weakness in their own personality. It is easy to over complicate such questions, as candidates are keen to hide or shield negative or weaker aspects of their character.

Biggest weakness

A common medical school interview question asks candidates to discuss their biggest weakness. Interviewers are looking for students to identify a genuine weakness and to have taken initiative to take steps to improve. The skill of reflection is critical in the development of a good doctor, and all doctors are required to reflect on their own abilities throughout their career. Medical school interviewers are keen to identify candidates who already reflect on their own skills and have acted upon this.

Step 1: Introduction The first step to answering a question about your biggest weakness is to provide a short introduction and set the scene to your answer. You should recognise the fact that everyone, no matter how skilled, will have a relative weakness alongside their strengths. Identifying weaknesses is critical for self-development and should not be shied away from.

Step 2: Identify a weakness The choice of weakness that you discuss is important. Take the time to reflect on your personality and pick a **genuine** weakness to discuss. Try to avoid cliché responses including perfectionism as a negative quality.

Expert's Advice

When discussing a personal weakness try and use the past tense where the question allows. This emphasises to the interviewers that you have since developed and improved the skill from the point in time that you identified it as a weakness.

Step 3: Discuss the process of development After recognising a weakness, you should aim to illustrate the steps taken to progress and develop that specific area or skill. This may include talking to teachers, asking for feedback, watching tutorials or reading articles to learn improvement methods. Detail the steps you took and how these have helped you.

Step 4: Show positivity Finally, frame the discussion in a positive light and turn the initial weakness into a current strength. Acknowledge that, while it has taken effort to improve, because of your efforts the skill that was once a struggle is now a personal asset. Illustrate this by using an example where you have used that particular skill and thrived doing so.

Sample responses

"I tend to be quite bad with my decision making, for example I underestimate the time taken to complete a task. In the past this has led me to take on too many tasks and I have struggled to complete them as I run out of time."

<u>Feedback</u> This is a poor answer. The student is overly negative about their weakness and this may lead the admissions   panel   to   conclude   that   they   would   struggle   with   the   demands   of   a   medical

course. The student could avoid this by adding examples of how they have developed or overcome their weak decision making skills.

"I can sometimes manage my time too ambitiously meaning I take on too many responsibilities which in turn leads to stress. For example, last year I took part in the school enterprise scheme, played rugby and ran my school's Medical Society. I ended up not having enough time to enjoy my time in each role and I spread myself too thin."

<u>Feedback</u> The weakness selected by this candidate is a good choice. It comes across as genuine and the student is able to give an example. However, this answer fails to provide evidence of improvement. The student should discuss how they went about improving their difficulties with time management and the ways in which they are better now.

"My biggest weakness is my tendency to underestimate how long tasks will take me. In the past this has led me to taking on too many responsibility which has resulted in increased stress. For example, during Year 11 I was Head Boy at school, played rugby at county level, took part in the Young Enterprise scheme and ran my school's Medical Society. I found myself being spread too thin and I was concious of the impact it may have on my academics. To counter this I had a discussion with my Head of Year about my difficulties. He was very helpful and helped me to delegate some of responsibility and prioritise the most important tasks. Now, I make sure to schedule my time in advance and avoid taking on more tasks than I can manage to ensure I remain organised."

<u>Feedback</u> This is a much stronger answer. The student clearly details the steps they took to address their weakness. As a result the student comes across as proactive and showing initiative.

Talking about strengths

An interviewer may ask you to describe your greatest strengths or attributes. These questions are far easier to answer compared to questions about weaknesses. The interviewer is looking for you to identify an appropriate, realistic strength aligned to a career in medicine. The best way to do this is to follow the Medic Mind framework for talking about skills to fully develop your answer and relate it to medicine.

Practice MMI station

> <u>Station brief</u> Describe a time where you made a mistake.

Good answer A good answer may include:

- Genuine, true and realistic example of a suitable mistake.
- Structured using the STARR approach.
- A positive approach, describing how the candidate used lessons from the mistake to improve themselves after reflecting on it.

Poor answer A poor answer may include:

- Description of a mistake that questions the candidate's suitability or professionalism, such as cheating on an exam.
- Overly negative or apologetic language without a focus on reflection and learning from the mistake.

4.8 Practice Questions: Personal Qualities & Skills

1. Why should we give you a place at our medical school?
2. What attributes do you have that will make you a good doctor?
3. Could you think of a situation where your communication skills made a difference to the outcome of a situation?
4. Are you an empathetic person?
5. Who has had a major influence on you as a person?
6. Give an example where you have played an effective role as a team member.
7. What makes you a good team player?
8. What makes you a good team leader?
9. Why is teamwork important in healthcare?
10. Do all teams need a leader?
11. What are the advantages and disadvantages of working in a team?
12. Are you a leader or a follower?
13. How do you manage your time?
14. What is the difference between empathy and sympathy?
15. How do you tackle criticism?
16. How would you give another medical student criticism?
17. How do you plan to overcome the challenges of medicine?
18. What personal qualities do you think you need to improve in order to be a better doctor?
19. How do you think other people describe you?
20. How would you cope with the death of a patient?
21. When do you seek out help with your academics?
22. Do you consider yourself a perfectionist? Why or why not?
23. Do you think academic or social intelligence is more important as a doctor?
24. What positions of responsibility have you held, and what did you learn from them?
25. Give an example of a situation where you have made a mistake and how you acted.
26. What is/was your favourite subject to study at school?
27. Give an example of a time where you showed resilience.
28. How do you tackle conflict?
29. Give an example of when you displayed good communication skills.
30. Do you think communication skills can be taught?
31. What skills are most important in a doctor?
32. Why is professionalism important in medicine?
33. Give an example of something that you had a strong opinion on but you changed your mind. What made you change your mind? How do you think now?
34. What do you think will be your greatest challenge in medicine?
35. Describe an event that you planned. Was it successful? How would you improve it?
36. Do you think doctors should "feel for their patients"?
37. What would you do if you were unsure of a patient's diagnosis?
38. What element of your personality would you like to change?
39. Why do you think you would be a good doctor?
40. What strengths would you bring to your group in a problem-based learning session?

CHAPTER 5

V Knowing the Medical School

5.1 Introduction

When you study medicine you are committing yourself to studying at a particular medical school for a period of several years. Universities are looking for you to have made an informed decision about not just becoming a doctor but also your choice of medical school. This means you are expected to have some degree of knowledge of each medical course and the teaching that is offered.

Common Pitfall

Prospective medical applicants are often guided to make 'strategic applications', by applying to schools they think they are most likely to recieve an offer from. Admissions panels will not see this as an acceptable reason for submitting an application. You should avoid any mention of statistics or the probability of success in your answers.

Talking about medical courses

Course structure - research the course structure and use this to answer questions about that specific medical school. Some of the points that could be raised when discussing each medical school are listed below.

Placement locations During your medical degree you will undertake placements at various different hospitals. The geographical area covered by each medical school can be quite varied and include some interesting placements. For example, Southampton students can be sent to islands such as Jersey, whereas Aberdeen students may be placed in rural highland regions.

Hospital specialisms Some medical schools are affiliated with specialist hospitals or hospitals containing unique wards. For example, students at UCL have the opportunity to undertake placements at the Royal Free which is home to the UK's only high level isolation unit. It is a good idea to research the medical school's main hospitals and take note of any unique or interesting departments that tie into your own interests.

Patient demographics The varying locations and types of hospitals that students are placed in during their degree has a direct influence on the demographics of patients seen during placements. For example, St George's is located in Tooting which has a very diverse population from a range of different socioeconomic backgrounds.

Timing of patient contact The point at which medical students meet their very first patient differs considerably among medical schools. In traditional medical schools, patient contact is often delayed until the clinical phase several years after they first began studying. However, in recent years there has been a shift towards earlier patient contact and it is now not unusual to take place even in the first year of medical school. Ensure to research the timing of placements and clinical contact for the courses you apply for, and consider any benefits and disadvantages that you could discuss in an interview.

Other opportunities Medical school offers students a wealth of opportunities beyond acquiring a medical degree. Some universities offer the opportunity to study an intercalated degree, meaning students can obtain an additional qualification in an area of interest at BSc or Masters level. Intercalation can be compulsory or optional depending on the medical school. Similarly, some courses may offer student selected units (SSUs) where medical students can opt to study one of a wide range of related subjects. Both intercalation and SSUs allow students to direct and shape their studies according to personal interests. If you have a particular passion or are excited to explore a specific area of medicine, mentioning this in the context of these opportunities will show you have thought about your future at that medical school.

Expert's Advice

Pay careful attention to how the medical school markets themselves. Carefully read the website or any other promotional information and take note of the key selling points that they have chosen to highlight. These points are likely the areas of the course that the medical school think are the most attractive. Try to incorporate these points into your answers where possible.

5.2 Teaching Styles

You may have noticed that there are differences in the teaching styles offered across medical schools. Before your interview make sure to research the medical school's syllabus and find out about the type of course they offer.

It is very common to be asked about the medical school's curriculum in your interview. It is expected that consideration of teaching style will have been a key factor in your decision to apply to that particular medical school. The interviewers are looking for you to be knowledgeable about their curriculum and to demonstrate that you are well suited to the style of teaching.

Common Pitfall

Remember to explain to the interviewer why your skills complement the curriculum. You need to convince the panel their teaching style is well fitting to you. Avoid simply listing elements of the curriculum without explaining why each aspect would benefit your learning overall.

Problem-based learning

Problem-based learning (PBL) is a teaching method used by a large number of medical schools. It places the student at the center of their own learning with a greater degree of independence and responsibility. PBL is primary taught through small group sessions of around 8-10 students who will discuss a particular problem or area of learning and identify relevant learning objectives. The group will then devise a plan to meet the learning objectives and solve the original problem. A tutor will also be present to facilitate the session and ensure students remain on track.

PBL courses encourage students to take control of their own learning and require self-motivation. One of the main benefits is the degree of independence and responsibility which helps develop confidence in dealing with clinical scenarios. PBL additionally builds key teamwork, communication and leadership skills from the very beginning of the degree so that students are prepared for clinical placements.

Sample responses

Why do you want to study a PBL course?

"I assume that PBL will provide a good mixture of lectures and small group sessions which will really help me. I sometimes struggle to concentrate in long lessons or lectures so I think I will be more suited to a group learning environment."

Feedback This answer is too negative. The candidate places too much emphasis on why lectures would **not** suit them rather than why PBL **will** suit their learning style. This may lead the interviewer to question if the student would struggle to cope with the demands of the course.

"I find self-directed work extremely rewarding as I feel that I am better suited to learn getting hands on with case studies. This is because I find it much more engaging and interactive compared to learning from a textbook   or   attending   large-scale   lectures."

<u>Feedback</u> This answer uses the same key points but is framed more positively. The student focuses on the aspects of PBL where they would thrive. This comes across as more positive and optimistic than the previous answer, and as a result the student appears enthusiastic and self-motivated.

Expert's Advice

As with other types of questions, try and use examples from previous studies to provide evidence for your main points. For example, reflecting on a school group project where you performed well and drawing comparisons to a PBL session will help convince the admissions panel you are well suited to their curriculum.

Case-based learning

Case-based learning (CBL) is similar to the PBL teaching style, focusing on small group learning to promote independence and self-direction. CBL tends to have a more clinical focus and is centered around a series of patient cases. The cases act as 'triggers' to stimulate interest and questions around areas of the curriculum, which can be explored in groups. A key difference from PBL is that CBL is typically more structured and provides learning objectives from the beginning of each case.

Sample response

What attracted you to apply specifically to this course?

"One thing I noticed was that you use Case-Based Learning, which is something I am really looking forward to. I believe the use of cases in the curriculum will enable me to get into the mindset of a future doctor, considering all the investigations and management that need to be made to take care of a patient. It will help me get into the routine of a differential diagnosis that will benefit me when I approach the clinical aspects of my medical training."

<u>Feedback</u> This answer demonstrates an understanding of how the skills developed by CBL are relevant to the work of a doctor. The candidate focuses on the future and shows elements of forethought and reflection.

Traditional learning

A traditional medical degree will split learning between 2-3 years of pre-clinical study followed by 3 clinical years. During the pre-clinical phase, student focus on learning the basic scientific disciplines of medicine such as physiology, biochemistry, and anatomy. This is typically delivered by traditional lectures and there is very little, if any, clinical exposure. The clinical phase marks the transition to full-time placements where much of the teaching takes place in a clinical setting, such as ward rounds or GP placements.

A benefit of the traditional approach is that it allows students time to build a strong foundation of medical knowledge, before applying the theory to real patients. This style may be more suited to students with strong scientific interests and those who are interested in pursuing researching alongside clinical work.

Sample responses

Do you feel that you would be missing out on an opportunity to maximise your learning since our medical school takes a more traditional approach, as compared to other courses which may use more modern techniques such as PBL?

"I don't really mind what type of teaching I have as at the end of the day all medical degrees will qualify you to work as a doctor. I feel assured in my own ability to adapt to different learning methods as I am very flexible. I plan to take the challenges of a traditional course in my stride."

<u>Feedback</u> This is a poor answer. The student fails to identify any benefits of a traditional course structure and does not seem to have done any research on the course. Medical schools will have put a lot of thought into the design of their course and want to see that applicants have carefully considered the benefits and challenges before applying.

"Not at all. I prefer independent study, as I feel I can pace my learning to suit my needs and combine it with resources that suit me such as visual aids and diagrams. While I agree that PBL can often help medical students gain skills to become a successful doctor, I prefer the clear structure of a traditional course."

<u>Feedback</u> This candidate shows and understanding of the benefits of a traditional course. They also apply this to their own learning style and preferences.

Integrated learning

An integrated course overlaps pre-clinical and clinical learning, often with early clinical contact in the first year. This enables students to contextualise pre-clinical theory by relating knowledge of basic medical science to the patients they meet. Integrated courses often use a systems-based approach whereby each body system (cardiovascular, renal, respiratory and so on) are studied in turn.

Integrated courses may also utilise a spiral-based curriculum. This describes how students revisit core concepts in each year of the course, gradually increasing the amount of clinical detail and complexity.

Sample responses

Why do you think the course at this medical school suits you?

"After reading your prospectus, I noticed that you have integrated learning. I really feel this will benefit me as it will have a mixture of different learning methods. I wasn't sure which teaching style would suit me best so decided to apply for integrated courses as it seems like a good middle ground."

<u>Feedback</u> This is a poor answer. The student comes across as unsure and uncommitted to the medical school. There is little reflection on their own skills or learning style, and this does little to convince the interviewer that they would be a good fit for their medical school.

"I really like how the course here is integrated, which means that I will benefit from a clear structured approach but also gain the benefits of problem based learning. This will enable me to gain a variety of skills including engaging in peer-learning and problem solving but also be able to pace my

learning. I tend to prefer independent study at school and I am looking forward to using this to my advantage in your curriculum."

<u>Feedback</u> This is a better answer. The student has clearly researched the course and comes across as excited and enthusiastic. They also demonstrate a degree of reflection through the recognition of how an integrated learning style will enable the development of relevant skills such as problem solving.

Other style of learning

Medical schools are constantly updating their curriculum and new teaching styles are emerging each year. For example, in recent years some universities have introduced evidence-based learning (EBL) and team-based learning (TBL) methods.

Regardless of the teaching style, remember to thoroughly research the course structure and prepare a handful of key benefits ready to discuss at interview. You should do this for each individual medical school and be specific to each course.

5.3 Dissection and Prosection

Anatomy is taught during the pre-clinical phase of a medical degree. The topic of anatomy is taught in a variety of ways with a surprising amount of variation in teaching methods between UK medical schools. Anatomy is traditionally one of the toughest aspects of medicine for first-year students, so it is worth researching the teaching at your chosen universities before attending an interview.

Expert's Advice

Anatomy teaching is not a topic that needs to be brought up at every medical school interview. Only mention it if this is an area you are particularly interested in, or if the medical school you are applying to has an interesting approach to teaching.

Dissection

Cadaveric dissection is the traditional method of teaching anatomy to medical students. It involves cutting the human body to reveal anatomical structures to aid learning. Medical schools utilising dissection will expect medical students to carry out the dissection themselves, often in small groups, using donated human cadavers.

Dissection is a very hands-on approach and allows students to see, physically touch, and explore organs to further their learning. This approach may appeal to budding surgeons as it provides early exposure to similar tools and techniques used in surgery to manipulate organ tissue.

Prosection

In contrast to traditional dissection, prosection involves students examining pre-prepared cadaveric samples. This means all of the cutting and dissection is performed by trained anatomists instead of students themselves. The major advantage of this is the high quality of dissection which can make it easier to identify important structures.

Prosection is becoming increasingly favoured by medical schools, as it is a more time efficient method of teaching. Students also have the opportunity to examine samples from multiple cadavers and can more easily gain an appreciation of normal anatomical variations.

Sample responses

Do you think you will find cadaveric dissection useful?

"To be honest, I am scared of blood and so feel a bit nervous about having to see a dead body but I will try my best to overcome my fears. I also don't think that working with cadavers will be useful as doctors operate on living patients and not ones that have already died."

<u>Feedback</u> This is a poor answer. The student fails to appreciate the unique learning experience that dissection could provide. This leaves a negative and uninterested impression on the interviewer.

"Yes of course! I am a visual learner and find that reinforcing something I read in a textbook into a real-life example will enable me to consolidate information better. I also feel it provides a far better reflection of the complexity of the human body than drawn-diagrams do, as they represent an accurate representation of anatomical   *knowledge."*

<u>Feedback</u> This student is enthusiastic and shows the interviewer they have reflected on dissection and can see benefits for their learning. The answer is positive and focuses on the strengths of dissection.

5.4 Practice Questions: Knowing the Medical School

1. What interests you about the curriculum at this university?
2. How does this medical school differ from the other schools you have applied to?
3. Tell me about the course we offer here.
4. Why do you think a PBL course would suit you?
5. Do you know much about the city this university is located in?
6. How do you learn best?
7. Are there any aspects of the course that you are particularly looking forward to?
8. Are there any aspects of the course that you are not looking forward to?
9. Why do you think we chose to use a PBL style curriculum?
10. Why do you think we chose a traditional curriculum?
11. Why did you apply here?
12. How did you decide which medical schools to apply to?
13. Would you rather train in a small district hospital or a large teaching hospital?
14. Apart from studying the medical course, are there any aspects of university life that you're looking forward to?
15. How do you think teaching will be different at university compared to at school?
16. If you had to re-design the medical curriculum how would you do it?
17. Why would a traditional teaching style suit you?
18. Why does the location of this university appeal to you?
19. What are the advantages of attending this particular medical school?
20. What are the disadvantages of attending this particular medical school?
21. How much do you know about dissection?
22. How much do you know about prosection?
23. Would you rather learn anatomy through dissection or prosection?
24. What are the benefits of early patient contact?
25. If you were designing a medical degree, at what stage would you introduce clinical placements and patient contact?
26. Would you want to undertake an intercalated degree?
27. What are the benefits of studying medicine as a graduate?
28. How would you contribute to our medical school's community?
29. What does it mean when we describe our course as 'integrated'?
30. What are the benefits of a foundation year before medicine?

CHAPTER 6

VI Core Knowledge

6.1 Introduction

The National Health Service (NHS) is the publicly-funded healthcare system of the UK. If you attend medical school in the UK you will spend all of your clinical placements in NHS hospitals and general practices. Consequently, you will be expected to demonstrate an understanding of the NHS values and basic structure at your medical school interviews.

As with all healthcare systems, the NHS does have its own flaws and challenges. An understanding of these is also paramount to showing interviewers you have what it takes to succeed as a doctor working in the UK.

History of the NHS

The NHS was proposed by the Labour Government in 1946. The original brainchild of the post-war Health Minister, Aneurin Bevan, the NHS came officially into service through the National Health Service Act on 5 July 1948. It was the first time in the world that completely free healthcare was available on the basis of citizenship.

NHS Founding Principles

The NHS was founded on three core ideas, expressed by Bevin at the NHS launch.

1. The NHS should meet the needs of everyone.
2. The NHS should be free at the point of delivery.
3. The NHS should be based on clinical need, not the ability to pay.

Now, over 70 years later, these three principles have guided the development of the NHS and remain at its core. The overall aim is to provide a comprehensive service, available to all irrespective of sex, race, disability, age and ability to pay.

6.2 NHS Structure

The NHS is a large and complex organisation which can be difficult to understand. It is made up of a wide range of different organisations, which span various roles and responsibilities. At a medical school interview, you are not expected to have full knowledge of every aspect of NHS structure. However, you should be prepared to answer basic questions about the workings of the NHS.

Primary Care

Primary care is central to the NHS. It represents the first point of contact for people who need healthcare. This includes GPs, dentists, sexual health clinics, pharmacies and drop-in centres. Primary care acts as 'gatekeepers' to the healthcare service and are able to refer patients to further services if necessary.

GPs are run as small independent businesses that are contracted to the NHS. They see the vast majority of patients, managing acute and chronic health conditions including mental health problems. Most general practices are run by a GP partnership, which usually involves two or more GPs working as business partners and owning a stake in the practice business. All the GP partners are jointly responsible for fulfilling the NHS contract for their practice, and in return they share any profit it generates.

Clinical Commissioning Groups

Clinical commissioning groups (CCGs) are were created in 2013. They are led by an elected governing body of GPs and other clinicians such as nurses. CCGs are responsible for around two-thirds of the NHS budget and commission local healthcare services such as urgent and emergency care, elective hospital services and community care. This means they are responsible for deciding which healthcare services should be provided for their local area, and who each service should be offered to.

From mid-2022, CCGs are set to be replaced by integrated care systems (ICSs). These are partnerships of organisations that work together to deliver health and care services in each local area. The of ICSs is to reduce competition between care providers and encourage co-operation to provide the best possible care for patients.

NHS Trusts

NHS Foundation Trusts provide care commissioned by the CCG. This includes secondary care hospitals, ambulance services, mental health services, social care and primary care. Secondary care refers to services provided by healthcare professionals that are not the first contact with a patient. For example, a patient with chronic disease may be referred to a specialist gastroenterologist who is based at the local hospital. Patients with complex or rare disease may need to be referred by secondary care doctors to specialist services or hospitals. This is known as tertiary care.

The Department for Health

The Department of Health and Social Care is the government department responsible for creating policy relevant for healthcare. They set the overall national strategy and allocate the NHS budget. The Department is led by the Secretary of State for Health and Social Care. As of 2022, the NHS budget was approximately £192 billion. This money comes from general taxes, national insurance and people using NHS services as private   patients.

Care Quality Commission

The Care Quality Commission (CQC) is an independent agency that monitors the quality of healthcare. The CQC regularly inspects the safety and quality of care in hospitals, general practices and care homes. Its findings are published and made publicly available. If NHS trusts do not meet certain standards, the CQC can issue warnings or place a practice into special measures.

6.3 NHS Constitution

In 2011, the Department of Health published the NHS Constitution which aims to establish the principles and values of the NHS. It details seven key principles underpinned by the original founding values.

1. The NHS provides a comprehensive service available to all.
2. Access to NHS services is based on clinical need, not an individual's ability to pay.
3. The NHS aspires to the highest standards of excellence and professionalism.
4. The patient will be at the heart of everything the NHS does.
5. The NHS works across organisational boundaries.
6. The NHS is committed to providing best value for taxpayers' money.
7. The NHS is accountable to the public communities and patients that it serves.

NHS Values

The NHS values have been derived from consultation with patients, public and staff members to express values that aim to underpin everything the NHS does.

Expert's Advice

Consider each NHS value in turn and try to identify an aspect of your life, be it an extra-curricular, part of your work experience, or something else, where you have acted according to these values.

Working together for patients Patients should come first. The needs of patients, and the communities in which they live, should be more important than organisational boundaries. Furthermore, patients and their families should be fully involved in their care.

Respect and dignity Every person should be valued - not just patients, but their families, carers and staff members too. Every person should be treated as an individual with respect to their unique aspirations and commitments in life. NHS professionals should be honest and open about what they can and cannot do.

Commitment to quality of care Every professional should strive to deliver safe, effective care every day. Feedback should be freely encouraged from patients, familiars, carers, staff and the public. This will enable the NHS to improve care and build on successes.

Compassion Compassion should be central to the care the NHS provides. They aim to respond with humanity and kindness to each person's pain, distress, anxiety or need. NHS professionals should search for things to do, however small, to give comfort or relieve suffering.

Improving lives The NHS strives to improve health and wellbeing. Excellence and professionalism make people's lives better, not only in clinical practice but in the everyday too.

Everyone counts The NHS makes sure that nobody is excluded, discriminated against or left behind. It is accepted that some people may need more help, that difficult decisions have to be taken and that when resources are wasted this results in wasted opportunities for others.

6.4 Training Pathways

Medical school is just the first step in your training to become a doctor. There are many different pathways you can take, and training can be different for everyone depending on your interests. Medical schools will expect you to have done some research into medical training so that you can make an informed decision about becoming a doctor. In this section, we explain some of the key aspects of medical training to be aware of.

Foundation Programme

After medical school, you will complete a two-year foundation programme covering a broad range of specialties across six 4-month rotations. Doctors in the foundation programme are known as FY1 (foundation year 1) and FY2 (foundation year 2) doctors. The aim is to give training in basic clinical skills across different settings. Successful completion of the foundation programme is necessary to apply for speciality training.

Medical Training

Medical training takes a similar structure to surgical training. After the foundation programme, doctors wishing to pursue a medical specialty will complete core medical training. This is a two or three-year programme in which trainees rotate through various medical specialties to learn to manage patients with acute and chronic medical problems. During core medical training, doctors take exams to qualify for Membership of the Royal College of Physicians to enter specialist training.

Specialist medical training allows you to qualify in a medical specialty such as cardiology, respiratory medicine, gastroenterology and many more. Application into specialty training is competitive and is assessed through a portfolio of achievements and interview. Specialty training varies in length and can last up to four years. Some specialties may require trainees to additionally train in general internal medicine at the same time.

Surgical Training

After foundation years, doctors can continue training in a specialist area such as surgery. Core surgical training is a two-year programme with 4-6 months spent in different surgical specialties. Trainees are also expected to study for, and pass, their membership exams for the Royal College of Surgeons.

Following core surgical training, after successful completion of your core surgical competencies, trainees can apply for specialty training. Specialty training is five-years and allows training in a specific area of surgery, such as urology, colorectal, or general surgery among others. Some surgeons opt to take time out for research or pursue a PhD too.

Run-through Programmes

A number of specialties have run-through training programmes. This means you train in your chosen specialty training straight after foundation training, without core medical or core surgical training. These specialties include paediatrics, obstetrics & gynaecology, psychiatry, radiology and others. The training structure and pathway differs between each specialty and can last up to seven years.

General practice Training

To qualify as a general practitioner, doctors apply to enter GP training following their foundation years. The GP training pathway is three-years long and involves placements in both primary and secondary care.

6.5 NHS Scotland

The NHS is a devolved system - meaning that the healthcare systems in each of the four UK countries are separate. While they are based on similar principles, if you are applying to a medical school in Scotland, it is important to have an understanding of the key differences between NHS Scotland and NHS England.

Similarities with NHS England

Just like the other UK countries, healthcare in Scotland is publicly funded through taxation and is free at the point of delivery. This means that financial means should not be a barrier to accessing healthcare anywhere in the UK.

Differences with NHS England

Unlike NHS England, NHS trusts do not exist in Scotland. Instead, healthcare is provided through fourteen regional health boards. These health boards hold much of the same responsibilities as English NHS trusts, and provide direct delivery of secondary care to each local population. There are also differences in funding, with the Scottish NHS receiving slightly more funding per person.

The Scottish Ambulance Service is the single public emergency ambulance and pre-hospital service for the whole of Scotland. This is in contrast to England where ambulance services are provided by ten regional NHS Ambulance Trusts.

One of the most noticeable differences, particularly for patients, is the lack of prescription costs in Scotland. In England a single prescription costs £9.35 per item, with no charge given for certain chronic illnesses and contraception. However, in Scotland every prescription is free of charge regardless of age group, disability or health condition. This is estimated to cost the Scottish NHS approximately £57 million per year.

6.6 Practice Questions: Core Knowledge

1. If you could meet anyone in the history of medicine, who would it be and why?
2. In your opinion, what has been the most important medical development in the past 50 years?
3. In your opinion, what has been the most important medical development in the past 100 years?
4. Can you tell me about the founding principles of the NHS?
5. What is the NHS Constitution?
6. Do you have any plans after medical school?
7. What is a junior doctor?
8. What is a registrar?
9. What is a consultant?
10. How do doctors train in the UK?
11. How is the NHS structured?
12. What is a CCG?
13. Can you discuss some similarities and differences between the NHS in Scotland and the NHS in England?
14. What are some of the biggest health issues in Scotland today?
15. What is the role of the NHS in today's society?
16. What is the biggest challenge, in your opinion, to the NHS at the moment?
17. How could we save money in the NHS?
18. How do you become a surgeon in the UK?
19. How do you become a GP in the UK?
20. How do you become a psychiatrist in the UK?
21. How is general practice different to hospital medicine?
22. Where does the funding for the NHS come from?
23. If you were Health Minister, what one thing would you change about the UK healthcare system?
24. Pick one core NHS Value. Why is this value important?
25. Why do you want to work for the NHS?
26. What do we mean by the terms 'primary care', 'secondary care' and 'tertiary care'?
27. What is the role of NHS Trusts?
28. What do you think are the problems with the way the NHS is structured?
29. How should the NHS budget be divided?
30. In your opinion, what is the main challenge faced by today's NHS?

CHAPTER 7

VII Medical Ethics

7.1 Pillars of Medical Ethics

Medical ethics have changed considerably over the last century, largely shaped by significant legal cases. Despite this fluidity in ethical definitions, 4 fundamentals have remained at the core of the profession. These form the pillars of medical ethics and underpin decision making in complicated scenarios.

The 4 pillars of medical ethics are as follows:

1. Autonomy
2. Beneficence
3. Non-maleficence
4. Justice

Just as with the SJT portion of the UCAT, understanding these concepts is vital to a successful medical interview. Regardless of format or institution, one must expect ethical scenarios to be tested in the interview. Often, this will be in the form of a scenario to which you must respond. In some cases, however, you may have to role-play; this will be discussed in other chapters. Questions will rarely ask interviewees to distinguish between ethical pillars. Rather, there is an expectation that stellar candidates will explore relevant ethics to the given scenario. For these questions, it is necessary to both, name and evaluate, the aforementioned ethical pillars within the context of the scenario. To do so, you must first understand each of these concepts.

Autonomy

> Autonomy describes the right of competent adults to make informed decisions about their own medical care.

In medical practice, autonomy is typically expressed as the right of a patient to take charge of decision making related to their own health, specifically as it relates to declining treatment. For example, if a doctor needs to take a blood sample from a patient, the reasons for and risks of this must be explained to the patient and a competent patient is consequently allowed to refuse.

Given the practical, legal and ethical significance of respecting autonomy, it is important to understand the nuances of autonomy.

Firstly, the principle underlies the requirement to seek the consent or informed agreement of the patient before any investigation or treatment takes place. Legally, an adult patient who suffers from no mental incapacity has an absolute right to choose whether to consent to medical treatment, regardless of whether this might be seen as sensible. It exists notwithstanding that the reasons for making the choice are rational, irrational, unknown or even non-existent.

Two conditions are ordinarily required before a decision can be regarded as autonomous.

1. The individual has to have the relevant internal capacities for self-government and has to be free from external constraints.
2. The individual has sufficient information to make the decision and does so voluntarily.

Notably, a decision made under coercion should not be respected as it cannot be said to be theirs. A common example may be that of an unsure young woman visiting a GP with her partner for a termination of a pregnancy. Whilst this may be entirely innocent, it is also the perfect breeding ground for coercion and abuse and it is good practice to spend time alone with the patient in order to confirm that the decision is truly theirs. In an interview, this concern should be stated.

Another important consideration regarding autonomy is that it does not apply bidirectionally. Whilst a patient can deny treatment, they cannot request or demand specific treatments.

Finally, all patients who are deemed to lack capacity must be treated in their best interests, unless prior legal documentation - such as a power of attorney - states otherwise. This also includes children under a certain age.

Expert's Advice

The line gets blurry when considering the role of autonomy as it applies to minors. We recommend perusing the 'Fraser Guidelines' and understanding Gillick Competence to better understand this niche. This must be applied to any ethical scenario involving minors under 16 years of age; common examples of this include requests for abortion and/or contraceptives.

Related jurisdiction

- Lord Donaldson. Re T (Adult) [1992] 4 All ER 649.

Beneficence and Non-Malefecince

Beneficence is to ensure that an action that is done, is done for the benefit of others. Non-maleficence means to "do no harm".

These two pillars often go hand-in-hand as they describe compatible concepts. Together, they state that medical professionals must work in a manner that maximises the benefit towards their patient. This is in keeping with the Hippocratic Oath, a philosophy with which most are familiar.

Examples of these may include a doctor refusing to perform an operation under non-sterile conditions as this would cause harm to the patient. Here, the doctor is acting in a way that benefits their patient whilst also preventing harm.

However, often, this principle may be confusing to clinicians as many beneficial therapies also have serious risks; a commonly encountered example is Chemotherapy in the treatment of Cancer. The pertinent issue, here, is whether the benefits outweigh the risks. To do so, a few considerations must be kept in mind.

1. Clinicians must not provide ineffective treatments to patients as they offer risk.
2. Doctors must not do anything that would purposely harm patients without the action leading to benefit that is proportional.

Justice

Justice encompasses the idea that the burdens and benefits of new or experimental treatments must be distributed   equally   among   all   groups   in   a   society.

Examples of this may include the provision of cancer treatments to non-smokers and smokers alike. This should be adhered to despite personal or public opinion about the role that smoking has played in their diagnosis of cancer.

Justice, ultimately, refers to the consideration of the law and overall benefit to society and involves the consideration of discrimination, human rights and legality.

The lines of justice were particularly blurred during the COVID-19 pandemic and there are a plethora of resources that further explain how this historic natural disaster molded the definition of a significant pillar of medical ethics.

Expert's Advice

Do not forget about the other ethical principles! It is easy to solely consider the 4 pillars as they are often brought up in discussions about the interview. However, there are many other ethical principles, such as confidentiality and consent, that are equally important and must be discussed in your responses.

7.2 Confidentiality

Whilst not a part of the pillars of medical ethics, confidentiality is an extremely important concept to consider in both, medical interviews and clinical practice. This is because it helps build trust in the doctor-patient relationship and improves public confidence in our profession. More importantly, confidentiality is a human right and helps prevent exploitation.

There are some scenarios wherein medical professionals can break confidentiality. Always ensure that the plan to break confidentiality is mentioned to the patient; this should be discussed in interview responses if you mention breaking confidentiality.

- **The patient is a danger to themselves.** Patients who are at an immediate risk of self-harm or suicide must be referred to psychiatric services.
- **The patient is a danger to others.** Doctors may break confidentiality by cooperating with the police in cases where a patient has been violent or committed an act of terrorism.
- **The patient does not communicate their HIV status to their partner**. As aforementioned, doctors may contact anyone at risk of infection directly if the patient refuses to do so.
- **A child is at risk of physical or sexual abuse or neglect.** This must be referred to the safeguarding team immediately.
- **Notification of specific infectious diseases.** Some communicable diseases, such as Malaria or Measles, are notifiable. Public Health authorities must be made aware of these to track transmission.

7.3 Consent and Capacity

To understand and apply rules around consent and capacity in medical interviews, it is vital to first understand the difference between the two terms.

Consent

This refers to an *act of reason* and means that a person must give permission prior to any act that might be performed to or on them, including any medical treatment, test or examination.

Informed Consent is a subset of this term and is vital to emphasize on in medical interviews. This refers to an information-based consenting process where the person giving their consent is doing so after assimilating all necessary information about the procedure to which they are consenting.

Capacity

This is a functional term referring to the mental or cognitive ability to understand the nature and effects of one's acts. One needs capacity to give consent.

Competence

This is a legal term often confused with the two aforementioned terms and refers to the requirement for healthcare professionals to perform functional tests of capacity to examine a person's ability to give consent.

Expert Advice

Consent and Capacity are concepts that are vital to consider in any ethical scenario. Therefore, we strongly recommend delving into this in any ethical interview question as it will show your admissions team that you are prioritizing the human right to consent in any and all situations.

Sample Responses

> Sergio, 13, is in hospital and requiring an urgent blood transfusion. His parents are happy for him to have it and the medical team strongly recommended the treatment. Sergio, however, is refusing based on an article he read online about the unethical nature of blood transfusions. Sergio is being stern and is not able to be persuaded. How should a medical team proceed?

"The problem at hand here is that a patient, who is noted to be a minor, is refusing an urgent medical procedure despite it being in his best interests. In this case, Sergio's autonomy and ability to consent must be balanced with the medical team's duty of beneficence and non-maleficence. Since he is only 13 years old and we have consent from his caregivers, the medical team can perform the blood transfusion. This is because as a minor, his competency is yet to be 100% confirmed and so he cannot be assumed to have capacity to deny treatment."

Feedback

This is a very good answer that touches upon the main ethical considerations in the scenario before acknowledging the patient's competency and responding accurately that he cannot deemed to have capacity. The only addition that can be made to further ameliorate this answer is to discuss

HOW the transfusion can be given since the patient disagrees with it. One can discuss communication techniques and the importance of empathy and emotional intelligence in speaking to Sergio to convince him otherwise.

Expert Advice

A good structure to rely on for ethical scenarios is to begin by describing the problem and the ethical considerations that define it. Following this, explore various responses and select the most appropriate one with reasoning. Finally, if time permits, discuss how the most adequate response can be actioned. In many cases, these questions will also lend themselves to personal reflection so feel free to explore any work experiences that may mimic the situation explored in the given scenario.

7.4 Abortion

An abortion refers to the medical process of ending a pregnancy so that it does not result in the birth of a baby.

Under the Abortion Act, abortions in England, Scotland and Wales can be carried out legally and safely before 24 weeks of pregnancy. Abortions can be carried out after 24 weeks in certain circumstances but the legalities that surround this are complicated and far beyond the scope of medical interviews.

Two doctors must agree that the abortion is less damaging to a women's mental or physical health than continuing the pregnancy. Furthermore, the procedure can only be carried out in a hospital and licensed clinic.

Regardless of your personal views surrounding the topic, candidates must explore arguments for and against any debate topic in medical interviews.

Arguments for Abortion

- Women's autonomy
- Beneficence
- Non-maleficence (mother)
- Non-maleficence (child)

Arguments against Abortion

- Autonomy of unborn child
- Unclear boundaries of gestational age for legal abortions
- Non-maleficence

Expert's Advice

We recommend bolstering your argument with an extra point in favor of, or against, the topic at hand given your final stance. For example, to debate in favor of abortion, state 3 arguments for it and 2 against before stating your final conclusion. This shows a balanced debate style and will be marked highly in the interview.

Namely, for interviews, be aware that medical professionals CAN deny abortions based on their personal views on the subject. However, they cannot virtue-signal their patients and must provide access to resources that will help the women in question.

Finally, appreciate that abortion is a complex issue, like euthanasia and establish that this is a complex situation with a lot of gray areas. Acknowledging this in the interview is vital.

7.5 Organ Donation

Organ Donation Laws are incredibly complex, region-specific and ever-changing. At a medical school interview level, only a basic understanding of organ donation schemes and organ allocation is required. In particular, strong candidates will be able to list key factors that are considered in allocating organs as well as a good basis of knowledge about the opt-in and opt-out schemes.

Opt-in Organ Donation

This is a system wherein members of the public are not automatically considered to be a part of the organ donor registry. Instead, interested patients must choose to opt into the scheme and become an organ donor.

The UK does *not* have an opt-in organ donation scheme.

Arguments for opt-in:

- Autonomy: patients will be making an informed and known decision to donate their organs, thereby practicing autonomy.

Arguments against opt-in:

- Fewer organs: decrease in the number of organs available as people may not register as organ donors whilst alive for numerous reasons, including but not limited to, perceived logistical difficulty, religious reasoning etc.

Opt-out Organ Donation

The UK moved to an opt-out organ donation scheme in May 2020. In part, this was due to a lack of available organs that lead to preventable deaths of over 400 people per year on the organ donation waiting lists. In this system, everyone is assumed to be on the registry unless they actively opt-out.

Arguments for opt-out:

- Beneficence: As aforementioned, there will be more donations and so, more lives saved.

Arguments against opt-out:

- Logistical difficulties: It is often quite difficult to opt-out of the system and many do not know that their are on the registry automatically. Hence, some may be donating organs never having previously consented to this.

Factors in allocation an organ

Sample Station

You are part of the committee responsible for deciding the order of patients on a waiting list for a new liver. Currently, you are discussing three patients, aged 23, 40 and 77, who are all in need of a new liver. What factors are important in making your decision?

Good response

"The amount of organs available for transplant unfortunately do not reflect the number of individuals needing life-saving transplants. Therefore, the scenario described is an ethical dilemma that plagues medical professionals in the UK quite often. There are a number of factors that heavily influence who gets an organ. I find it useful to think of these in terms of clinical and sociological factors, though there may be an overlap between these categories.

Clinical factors include age, general health and biological match, amongst other things. For example, younger patients would generally live longer if given the liver transplant. They may also be in better health and therefore, more likely to survive major surgery. This lends to a higher saving of QALYs or Quality Adjusted Life Years.

Sociological factors, in the context of liver transplants, may be something like their alcoholism status. We would need to consider whether any of these patients have a history of alcoholism. Are they still drinking? Are they likely to ever abstain? This is important to consider as they may end up drinking again and damaging the new liver as well.

With these factors in mind, their ages are not enough data to make an adequate choice as to who would get their liver and I would need to consider the aforementioned factors before making a decision."

Bad response

"I think whoever gets the liver should be those that need it due to illnesses such as cancers or congenital issues. I would disagree that a liver transplant should be given to someone with a self-inflicted disease, such as alcoholism, as they are likely to keep drinking and damage the new liver."

This is an inadequate answer as it does not consider enough factors, such as in the good answer. Moreover, it comes across as judgmental and does not fall in line with NHS values of treating everyone equally, regardless of whether their illness is self-inflicted or not. Finally, in this answer, we can see that the response lends an immediate decision that does not focus on the multi factorial decision making processes that organ transplant decisions requires.

7.6 Euthanasia

Euthanasia is the act of deliberately ending a person's life to relieve suffering. For example, it could be considered euthanasia if a doctor intentionally gave a patient with a terminal illness an overdose of muscle relaxants to end their life.

Assisted suicide is the act of deliberately assisting or encouraging another person to kill themselves. For example, if a person obtained strong sedatives, knowing that their relative with a terminal illness intended to use it to kill themselves, this is called assisted suicide.

There are various types of euthanasia;

1. Voluntary: with informed consent of the patient being euthanized
2. Involuntary: without informed consent of the person being euthanized
3. Active: prescribing medication that will actively cause deterioration leading to death
4. Passive: withdrawing treatment such that it causes death

In the UK, active euthanasia and assisted suicide are both illegal. In other parts of the world, however, euthanasia laws are more flexible. For example, Switzerland and Germany allow assisted suicide and passive euthanasia but not active euthanasia. The latter is, however, legal in Belgium, Netherlands and Luxembourg.

Expert Advice

It is useful to know examples of countries where euthanasia laws differ from those in the UK as this can be used to strengthen arguments for or against the topic in interviews and shows a global understanding of healthcare laws.

Approaching the Euthanasia Debate in Medical Interviews

- **Don't be too strong.** Avoid making harsh arguments either for or against the topic. Instead, give balanced arguments that mirror the complexity of euthanasia debates.
- **Use the 4 pillars of ethics.** This will bolster your argument and lend ethical reasoning to your answer.
- **Use case studies.** Using case studies and examples from across the world shows a nuanced understanding of the topic and shows examiners that you are a well-read candidate.
- **Mental Capacity Act.** One of the biggest barriers to legalizing euthanasia is the fine line between accepting one's autonomy to die versus perceiving this intent to be a symptom of the mental stress caused by physical illness. Understanding whether a patient has capacity to request euthanasia is important.

Arguments for Euthanasia

1. Relieves the suffering of patients with terminal illnesses.
2. International availability means that patients with the means to, may access this abroad, thereby causing an equality divide in who is able to access euthanasia.
3. Respects the autonomy of a patient with a terminal illness.

Arguments against Euthanasia

1. Goes against the best interests of the patient with regards to keeping them alive.
2. Disrespects the ethical pillar of non-maleficence.
3. Difficult to comment on whether a patient's desire to die is caused by the mental health impact of their physical illness or an actual, informed desire to be euthanized.

7.7 Practice Questions

1. Do you believe that euthanasia should be allowed?

2. Why is confidentiality important?

3. Can confidentiality ever be broken. If so, when can it be?

4. Should doctors be allowed to strike?

5. Should doctors be allowed to protest?

6. You are part of a medical council deciding upon allocation for a liver transplant. There is one liver, but two patients. Patient A is a 75 year old war hero and non-drinker. Patient B is a an ex-alcoholic who is a lone parent at the age of 27. Who should get the organ?

7. Organ donation in the UK is currently via an opt-out system, whereby by default option is no donation. Discuss opt-out schemes, and other methods to increase donations of organs in the UK

8. A woman who is bleeding heavily refuses to receive a blood transfusion that you are proposing. Why do you think this might be? How would you handle the issue?

9. A man refuses treatment for a potentially life-threatening condition. What are the ethical issues involved?

10. Do you think that Class A drugs should be legalised?

11. Do you think it should be compulsory for doctors to report to the police if their patients use illegal drugs?

12. How do you respond and what do you feel when you see a beggar in the street?

13. What do you think about the use of animals for testing new drugs?

14. Should doctors have a role in contact sports such as boxing?

15. Do you think we should find out more about patients' views of their doctors, their illness or their treatments? How would you set about this?

16. Some Trusts are refusing to perform some elective operations on obese patients. Why do you think that it? Do you think it's right?

17. Is it right that Viagra should only be available to certain groups of men?

18. Would you perform abortions as a doctor?

19. What are some pros and cons of abortion?

20. What is your feeling about euthanasia?

21. Do you think the Hippocratic oath is outdated?

22. Would you prescribe the oral contraceptive pill to a 14-year old girl who is sleeping with her boyfriend?

23. Female infertility treatment is expensive, has a very low success rate and is even less successful in smokers. To whom do you think it should be available?

24. How do you think doctors should treat injury or illness due to self-harm, smoking or excess alcohol consumption?

25. With the growing problems of overpopulation should the NHS fund IVF treatment?

26. What is a doctor's role in ensuring a patient can give informed decision?

27. What are the ethical issues involved when a patient under 16 wants to refuse treatment?

28. What are the pros and cons of banning alcohol?

29. What are the four ethical pillars? Can you give examples when you have seen these in practice?

30. Do you think marijuana should be provided free to particular patients on the NHS?

31. Do you think alternative or complementary medicine should have an increased role in the NHS?

32. Should vaccines be made compulsory for medical students?

33. What would you do if a patient with an STI was refusing to tell their partner about their STI and plans to continue to have sex with this partner?

34. What issues would you consider when deciding to allocate an organ to a patient?

35. How would you react as medical student if a patient told only you private information and asked you not to tell anyone?

36. What would you do as a GP, if a 13 year old patient asked you for the contraceptive pill?

37. What would you do as a doctor, if you overheard someone on the phone in the supermarket having a conversation about their recent symptoms and you believed that they had cancer?

38. Do you think animal testing should be used for drug development?

39. Should doctors complain about their employer or colleagues on social media?

40. What consequences might a doctor face from whistleblowing?

CHAPTER 8

VIII NHS Hot Topics

8.1 COVID-19 Pandemic

When it comes to latest topics in Medicine, it is no surprise that the COVID-19 pandemic is a popular one. However, keep in mind that the pandemic is a changing topic. Typically, medical interview questions stand the test of time, but, for example, a station on the COVID-19 vaccine may look very different as new research and supply challenges emerge.

The pandemic is, of course, a broad topic so focus your reading on the following main aspects;

- Lock-downs and their efficacy
- Changes to clinical practice caused by COVID-19
- Science behind the popular vaccines (eg: Pfizer and Moderna)
- Fundamentals of RNA vaccines
- Ethics surrounding mandatory vaccines and/or lock-downs
- Socioeconomic inequalities uncovered by the pandemic
- Long-term challenges caused by the pandemic (eg: increased tele-medicine and it's impact on poorer communities, impact of virtual education on young children etc.)

Sample Station 1

How has the UK responded to the COVID-19 pandemic? Do you think it has been effective in reducing the number of cases seen in the UK? Why do you think the outcomes have been vastly different in other countries?

Good Answer:

- **Demonstrates knowledge.** Cites specific measures that the UK has taken to combat the COVID-19 pandemic. This can include lock-down measures, vaccine supply or NHS strategies.
- **Talks about what has worked.** Provides insight on protocols that have been effective in reducing case incidence.
- **Talks about what has not worked.** Hypothesises why implementation of measures has not brought case incidence down even more.
- **References statistics.** Uses statistics, articles, or data to bolster answer.
- **Identifies successful legislation.** Picks countries that have more successfully combated COVID-19 numbers i.e. New Zealand
- **Explores what worked.** Discusses why measures worked well in these places. Explores why the UK did not do the same.
- **Identifies unsuccessful legislation.** Picks countries that have less successfully combated COVID-19 numbers i.e. Brazil(2nd highest deaths to date)
- **Explores what did not work.** Discusses why measures did not work as well in these places, non-judgmentally.

This information can easily be gleaned off of government data that is freely available online. Understanding the course that the pandemic has taken in the UK, especially in comparison to other countries with similar population densities, showcases a highly academic and well-read candidate.

Bad Answer:

- **Vague.** Does not reference UK-specific measures that have been taken (lock-downs, tier system, etc.)
- **One-sided.** Talks too heavily about either what has worked or what has not worked.
- **Not enough insight.** Unable to apply personal insight to the information provided in the brief.
- **Tangential comments.** Relies too heavily on tangential topics related to the coronavirus pandemic as opposed to addressing the brief head-on.
- **Cannot identify countries with different outcomes.** Speaking vaguely about what could have been better/worse as opposed to using examples from other countries.
- **Poor exploration as to why.** Not exploring the difference between the UK and other countries and exploring why these differences make implementing government advice more/less challenging.
- **Judgmental.** Biased voicing of concerns in countries that manage COVID numbers differently than the UK.

Expert Advice

It is important to not only demonstrate knowledge of COVID-19 as a virus and its infectious potential in this station. It is equally important to discuss why the measures undertaken by the government have been enforced. In order to do this, consider the benefits of restrictions being as strict as they are and consider the hesitations in implementing stricter restrictions. This will show the interviewer you empathise with what a tricky balance this is to strike, and you come across as non-judgmental. Using ethical terminology, such as the 4 pillars, can help bolster your answer as well!

Sample Station 2

Discuss the ways in which the COVID-19 pandemic has affected the delivery of healthcare services in the UK. Which groups of people do you think have been particularly impacted?

Good Answer:

- **Resource reallocation.** Mentions more resources and staff being devoted to COVID management and fewer to other areas.
- **Impact on healthcare staff.** Considers additional burdens placed on healthcare staff. Mental health and worry of infecting loved ones or patients.
- **Impact on non-COVID patients.** Considers increased wait-times for particular services and poor prioritisation for non-COVID patients.
- **Impact on patients' families.** COVID patients are unable to have visitors due to the infectiousness of the disease.
- **Consider a variety of topics to discuss.** For example, fewer elective procedures (3.9 million fewer elective procedures April 2020- Aug 2021), delays in scans, diagnostics and treatments for cancer patients, increase in mental health diagnoses due to isolation, reduced support etc and stressful working conditions for NHS keyworkers.

- **Show understanding of inequalities in impact of COVID-19.** For example, the disproportionate impact the pandemic had on lower socioeconomic groups.

Bad Answer:

- **Does not reference resource reallocation.** Misses the first part of the brief and jumps into the second.
- **Fewer than two groups mentioned.** Mentioning one or fewer concrete groups that have been affected by these changes.
- **Lack of empathy.** Does not make efforts to empathise with the groups that have been negatively impacted by strained NHS services at this time.

Expert Advice

This station is fairly vague, which means that there are multiple directions in which a student can guide their response. While it's important to discuss more than one affected group, continue to elaborate about the topics you know more about (ex. immuno-compromised patients accessing hospital care), as interviewers will likely ask follow-up questions about the topics you bring up.

Sample Station 3

You are the head of the World Health Organisation. A new virus has just broken out in Mexico City. There are 154 cases in Mexico City, but no other cases to date elsewhere. Devise a strategy to prevent this virus becoming a pandemic.

Possible points to mention:

- **Quarantine individuals.** The individuals infected should be placed in a hospital where they cannot spread the infection.
- **Conduct research.** Medical teams need to find out the symptoms, incubation period, route of transmission of the virus, etc. Research should also focus on optimising treatment strategies and finding a vaccine.
- **Sequence the genome.** China quickly sequenced the genome of COVID-19 and released it to the WHO. This meant that the worldwide search for a vaccine could begin.
- **Release a briefing to world media**. This way, people in other countries can take measures to reduce transmission.
- **Invest in medical equipment.** Consider the equipment and facilities needed to manage the disease and invest in this.
- **Find the source.** Find the source to prevent transmission (ex. if it is from a particular food market, close the market).
- **Quarantine the city.** Mexico City (or the affected local area) may need to shut down. Advise people to stay indoors.
- **Possibly ban travel to/from Mexico City.** Limit travel to/from Mexico City, or Mexico, so as to prevent the cases from spreading to other cities or countries.
- **Encourage good hygiene.** Promote hand-washing, mask-wearing, covering mouth when sneezing/coughing. Disinfect public spaces regularly.

8.2 Brexit

Understanding the effects of Brexit on the NHS is key to answering questions that revolve around this topic. Keep in mind that Brexit has already taken place and so, it is vital to comment on perceived impact versus realized impacts of the separation on healthcare in the UK.

Scientific Research

- Loss of free movement for scientists
- Loss of EU funding

Employment

- Loss of European NHS workers
- Falling numbers of EU nurses applying for jobs
- Knock-on effect on other NHS workers

Pharmaceuticals

- Regulatory uncertainty
- Medical supply chains
- Lack of access to EU clinical trials

Access to treatment

- European Health Insurance Cards no longer valid in the UK or for UK citizens abroad
- Reciprocal healthcare

Extra funds

- Saving on EU membership fees
- EU citizens no longer entitled to free treatment

Remember to consider the perceived impact as stated above versus the ways in which these effects have manifested. Did they all happen? If so, where they positive or negative?

8.3 7-Day NHS

To understand the logic behind the 7-day NHS debate, we must first consider the statistics that drove this to be considered. This is known as the "weekend effect" and describes a collection of statistics showing poorer patient outcomes on the weekend, typically due to reduced services. Below are key statistics gleaned from the "weekend effect", as per the British Medical Journal.

- 15.9 million hospital admissions a year
- 1.8% of these patients die within 10 days of admission
- Patients are 15% more likely to die if admitted on a Sunday than a Wednesday
- Patients are 10% more likely to die if admitted on a Saturday than a Wednesday

Whilst these statistics are staggering at first sight, it is vital to thoroughly analyse them if mentioned in an interview. For example, consider the other factors that may play into these increased deaths, such as increased admissions, higher major trauma admissions etc.

Arguments against the 7-day NHS:

- **More stress.** It will lead to more stress for doctors, leading to poorer morale and worse efficiency.
- **More mistakes.** Tired doctors will make more mistakes.
- **Less desire to be a doctor.** There is already a growing negative stigma against some parts of the job of a doctor, so it could reduce applications.
- **Discussion of wages.** The NHS hasn't got funds to pay higher wages on weekends.

Arguments for the 7-day NHS

- **Patient care continuity.** Patients are less likely to get lost in the system due to regular working teams continuing on the wards over the weekend.
- **Lesser delays in patient care.** Regular service over the weekend would allow for more patient investigations and discharges without delay which would allow for a smoother and faster moving admissions list in hospitals.

Expert Advice

Don't be scared to think outside the box and try to actually provide a solution. For example, you could argue against a 7 day NHS, but state that if it does happen, there should be much higher wages for doctors to compensate. Consider other ways in which to meet patients' needs over the weekend without compromising staffing conditions.

1:1 MEDICINE INTERVIEW TUTORING

 Delivered by current Medicine students, who excelled in the interview themselves

 A personalised 1:1 approach, tailored to your unique needs

 An overall 93.4% success rate, with students improving their performance by an average of 57.3%

EXCLUSIVE OFFER: GET 70% OFF YOUR FIRST LESSON

Book a free consultation today to unlock this offer by visiting www.medicmind.co.uk/interview-tutoring/ or scan the QR code below

MEDICINE INTERVIEW ONLINE COURSE

 100+ tutorials, and 200+ MMI stations , designed by our Medicine interview experts

 Learn how to answer questions on motivation for Medicine, personal skills, work experience, hot topics, and more

 A range of packages available, including a live day of teaching and 1:1 tutoring

GET 10% OFF USING THE CODE 'BOOK10'

Find our more at www.medicmind.co.uk/interview-online-course/ or scan the QR code below

MEDICINE LIVE MMI CIRCUIT

 Written by real MMI examiners, and trusted by schools and the NHS

 Perform 10 live MMI stations yourself, completing a full circuit, and then pair up to observe an additional 10 stations!

 Experience a wide range of stations, covering role plays, medical ethics, NHS hot topics, work experience, and more

GET 10% OFF USING THE CODE 'BOOK10'

Find our more at www.medicmind.co.uk/medicine-mmi-course/ or scan the QR code below

CHAPTER 9

IX Virtual Interviews

9.1 Introduction to Virtual Interviews?

With the onslaught of the COVID-19 pandemic, multiple universities were forced to reconsider their typical admissions processes. Namely, this impacted medical interviews as they, inherently, did not follow the health and safety protocols demanded by the pandemic. As you have now learned, typical interviews occur in close quarters and with multiple interactions between people who have traveled from afar. Therefore, virtual interviews became the norm amongst all UK medical schools to help facilitate the admissions process.

Whilst the pandemic may no longer be in full force, many universities continue to offer virtual interviews as they allow for improved flexibility, particularly for applicants who may live farther away. They are also often easier and safer for the universities to run. Therefore, considering virtual formats for your interview is key despite reduced COVID restrictions.

Virtual interviews can be in an MMI or traditional format and typically occur on whichever video conferencing platform is used by the university for their day-to-day teaching. Common platforms include MS Teams and Zoom. Some MMI stations, like manual dexterity, were excluded from these interviews as they were not possible to perform on camera. However, most interview themes remained the same as those explored in previous chapters.

Whilst the underpinnings of the interview remain the same in a virtual format, the communication skills required to ace them are completely different. On camera, it is much harder to showcase the non-verbal communication skills that would otherwise form a large part of your assessment. Consequently, preparation and communication must be tailored to this new-age format of interviews.

9.2 Preparing for Virtual Interviews

Preparing for virtual interviews takes time, consistency and careful consideration of the variety of skills required to showcase your talents on-screen as opposed to in-person. Keep in mind that medical interviews are largely held to assess a candidates personality and emotional intelligence, both of which can be harder to showcase on a virtual platform. Consequently, tailoring your communication skills is key so keep the following pointers in mind in your preparation.

Expert Advice

If you are unsure as to whether your universities are hosting in-person or virtual interviews this year, ensure that you prepare for both; this is particularly important in the case of last-minute changes to interview circumstances.

Record yourself

Non-verbal communication skills can be very difficult to showcase virtually. Moreover, some non-verbal skills, such as hand gestures, can be done but need to be adapted for smaller screen spaces. We strongly recommend that applicants record themselves answering common interview questions, such as "Why Medicine?", and watch these recordings back to critique themselves. This can be done using the record function on any major video conferencing software, such as Zoom.

Upon watching the recording back, ensure you focus on aspects such as posture, facial expression and intonation as these tend to stand out more than others. For example, considering the previous example of hand gestures, these naturally happen quite low in which case it will not be caught on camera. So, virtually, you must ensure that you gesticulate higher up, almost at neck level, to ensure that you come across as engaging and enthusiastic even on camera!

Familiarise yourself with the necessary video conferencing platforms

Peruse the internet or contact your universities to find out which video conferencing platforms they use for their medical interviews. Practice using the same platforms so that you are familiar with the ways in which it works. Familiarity breeds confidence and this will help prevent unnecessary stressors on the day.

Adjust your timing

Virtual interviews will almost always have strict time limits, even more so than in-person MMIs or panels. Learn to keep your answers succinct yet engaging and reflective. This can often be the most difficult consideration for interviewees. Below are some quick and helpful timing tips to keep in mind when preparing for your interview.

1. Ask yourself WHY an admissions team might be interested in your answer. Applicants often misinterpret the reasoning behind a given question, thereby responding in a way that does not satisfy the university's requirement. By confirming the motivation behind a particular question, you can tailor your answer to delve into the points that are most important to them. A good example of this is questions that refer to work experience. This is typically included to ensure that students have a balanced idea of the career and so, tailoring your answer to focus on this will ensure you answer it efficiently.

2. Follow a strict structure for various question times. The STARR format is a good one to rely on for almost any station/question as it focuses on reflection. Structuring your responses will prevent you from scrambling around or including unnecessary details.

3. In a pinch, zoom in on your reflections as this is almost always the most highly valued part of any good answer. Ensure that your reflections are balanced!

Becoming camera-ready

Set up your video conferencing equipment far in advance of your interview and practice using this same set-up. This means finding a quiet, well-lit space with plain backgrounds, little distraction and a strong Wi-Fi connection. Additionally, find the right level to place your computer and play around with it's settings to ensure maximum video and audio quality.

Whilst it may seem like a minor detail, ensure you reflect on your clothing choices for the interview. Remember that stark white clothing, or alternatively, extremely bright and patterned clothing, does not showcase well on-camera as it disorients saturation and brightness. We recommend plain, darker colored clothing. Additionally, it may seem tempting to only dress formally on your upper half as this is what is noticeable on camera. However, dressing the part will help you feel more confident on the day and avoids any risk of a photo bombing bathrobe mid-interview.

Eye-contact

This is a tricky one as often, applicants are tempted to look at the screen during the interview. This, however, comes across as a lowered gaze from the other end. Consequently, practice avoiding on-screen distractions while focusing your eye-contact at camera-level. Recording yourself, as aforementioned, will help you fix this problem in real-time.

Use a cheat-sheet (if permitted)

Some universities allow students to use a cheat-sheet to help keep track of key points and ideas during the interview. Find out beforehand if this is permissible as it can help calm nerves to have set examples and reflections to fall back on when stuck. Make sure that you contact your university beforehand to find out if post-it notes, pens or paper are allowed during your interview. This is especially important because if they are not, you want to clear your desk of these items to prevent any misunderstandings during the interview.

Tidy up your virtual identity

It is not uncommon for applicants to have previous nicknames or ironic pictures on their Zoom or Teams profiles. Ensure that you double check your virtual identity prior to the interview. Opt for your full name and a clear, professional photograph as this speaks well to your interviewers even before they have met you!

Consider others

On the day of your interview, ensure that your family, friends and neighbors are aware. Double check prior to the interview that there are no planned roadworks or other construction in your area. If you live with young children or pets, ensure that you make alternate arrangements to care for them so that you are not interrupted. Most importantly, if interrupted, do not panic. Smiling, apologizing and laughing it off will showcase a strong, confident and personable applicant far more than reacting with anger or frustration.

Much of the preparation for virtual interviews, aside from the above pointers, remains similar to that for in-person MMIs or panels. Therefore, practicing this alongside the remainder of the advice in this book will help you ace virtual interviews.

CHAPTER 10

X Oxbridge Interview

10.1 Preparing for the Oxbridge Interview

10 Tips for Oxbridge Medical Interviews

Just getting invited to interview at Oxford or Cambridge is a considerable achievement in its own right, but it's no secret that Oxbridge interviews are amongst the hardest a prospective medical student might have to negotiate. Even so, there's plenty of preparation you can do to give yourself the best chance of success – here are ten of our recommendations.

Just getting invited to interview at Oxford or Cambridge is a considerable achievement in its own right, but it's no secret that Oxbridge interviews are amongst the hardest a prospective medical student might have to negotiate. Even so, there's plenty of preparation you can do to give yourself the best chance of success – here are ten of our recommendations.

Just getting invited to interview at Oxford or Cambridge is a considerable achievement in its own right, but it's no secret that Oxbridge interviews are amongst the hardest a prospective medical student might have to negotiate. Even so, there's plenty of preparation you can do to give yourself the best chance of success – here are ten of our recommendations.

1. Revise your science

Scientific aptitude is the single biggest factor by which Oxbridge interviewers assess medical applicants. Therefore, the best way to prepare is by getting 100% clued up on the relevant content of your A-Level science syllabuses. For Biology, that means practically everything but plant biology and ecology; for Chemistry, it's harder to know what to revise, but the fundamentals of physical, organic and inorganic chemistry could certainly all be relevant.

Thanks to the Supplementary Additional Questionnaire (SAQ), you shouldn't panic over topics you haven't covered yet, as it allows interviewers to tailor their questions to what you've been taught. That said, there are certain topics that simply won't be off-limits – think biological molecules or major organ systems, for example – ask your teacher to skip ahead if these are timetabled for after Christmas.

2. Make use of online information

Just because Oxbridge interviews are different from those at other medical schools, doesn't mean you have to guess in the dark as to what yours could be like. The two universities, not to mention specific colleges, provide plenty of information online about how they like to assess applicants, and you can even watch mock interviews for free. Additionally, there are numerous sources of interview questions that previous applicants have been asked – on forums and on the Medic Mind website!

3. Plug the gaps in your clinical knowledge

Your A-Level studies and general knowledge will already span most of the clinical cases that could come up for discussion in an Oxbridge interview. But if you've got niggling uncertainties about any of the big ones – heart attacks, Alzheimer's or an infectious disease, for example – it's worth doing a bit of research and making some notes. You don't want to get caught out!

4. Prepare for questions involving unseen analysis

Oxbridge interviewers like to challenge candidates to analyse the unseen – from data in graphs or tables to objects (such as bones) and medical images (scans or histological slides). They don't expect you to work out everything perfectly on your own and are more interested in seeing how you think and deal with the unexpected. However, if you've familiarised yourself with the basics of, say, how different bones are adapted for their functions, the process should be less intimidating.

5. Get suitable interview practice

You should try to organise at least one mock interview that imitates the Oxbridge substance and style – practice interviews for other medical schools probably won't be similar enough. You can organise these with anyone you know who studied medicine or biological science of any kind at Oxford or Cambridge. If you don't, though – as will be the case for most people – consider asking a member of the science department at school to try and replicate the interview experience for you.

6. Research your interviewers

Typically, a written invitation to interview will include the names of those interviewing you. Looking them up online won't tell you exactly what's going to come up (far from it), but it'll put a face to a name and – based on their research or clinical speciality – tend to offer a good indication of the broad line of questioning they'll pursue. Not only should this show you which topics to revise especially well, it'll help you feel more relaxed going into your interviews. But don't be thrown off if they ask about something totally different!

7. Practise delivering long answers

A great way for Oxbridge interviewers to see how your mind works is to ask open-ended questions that demand longer explanations with limited interjection on their part. How does the heart work? Or: what can you tell me about water?

A couple of points or sentences won't suffice here. So, build on your interview skills by posing such questions to yourself and improvising answers that cover at least four or five of the most significant points. You'll get more comfortable with the sound of your own voice, too, which is no bad thing.

8. Explore beyond the syllabus

Reading beyond the A-Level basics is a classic piece of Oxbridge preparation advice for any subject. It certainly remains true for medicine, although there's so much A-Level knowledge to test you on in the first place that you really don't need to go overboard with this. Mentioning the latest scientific or clinical research on a topic can be a good way to show your enthusiasm for medicine, but not if your understanding doesn't stand up to further questioning. A better strategy might be to read in more detail over specific areas of your A-Level course.

9. Set most of the usual prep to one side

One of the unique things about Oxbridge interviews is that they tend to ignore the staples of most other medical interviews – questions about why you chose medicine or their specific university, as well as questions on your personal statement, work experience or personal traits. For the vast majority of interviewees, none of these will come up. That's not to say you should tempt fate and ignore them entirely in the course of your preparation, but chances are that you will be able to answer these adequately with minimal prior work.

10. Don't worry over a question

It's typical for dons to close out an interview by inviting you to ask any questions you may have. Some applicants like to prepare off-the-syllabus questions intended as a show of intelligence. While this certainly won't harm your chances of success, it can be an unnecessary cause of stress. We advise doing what comes naturally to you – asking about something in the interview that's piqued your scientific interest; making honest enquiries about the course, college or university; or politely asking nothing at all.

10.2 Oxbridge Academic Scenarios

Oxbridge Medicine Interview: Academic Scenarios

The Oxford and Cambridge Medicine Interviews are notoriously difficult, and are quite different in style to your typical undergraduate medicine interview.

Oxbridge medicine interview questions tend to be more academic and challenging in general. They will tend to focus less on extracurricular activities ("e.g. how do you manage stress?") and personality questions (e.g. "give me an example of when you showed teamwork"), which are often staples of MMI interviews at most UK universities. Instead, Oxbridge interviewers will grill you on your interest and knowledge in science and medicine.

Preparing for an Oxbridge medicine interview can be quite overwhelming. The key thing to bear in mind is that you cannot know all of medicine before an interview – there is a reason you are an applicant not a qualified doctor! It can help to be aware of some common conditions and topical scientific topics, but do not stress too much about reading lots of textbooks on science and medicine.

Oxbridge interview questions will focus less on your knowledge, but instead on your ability to think outside the box and build on your knowledge

The Oxbridge medicine interview questions will focus less on your knowledge, but instead on your ability to think outside the box and build on your knowledge. For example, if a scenario focuses on Covid-19, the Oxbridge medicine interviewer may begin with some simple questions about Covid-19. They would expect you to understand the science behind the virus, some knowledge of viruses as organisms, and insight into the mechanism of vaccines. However, the conversation may soon lead to some rather tricky follow up questions into areas of science you have never come across before. The key is not to panic in your Oxbridge medicine interview, as the scenario is often not testing your knowledge, but instead your ability to use the little knowledge you do have to make logical assumptions and conclusions.

In this article we have some mock Oxbridge interview scenarios. We would recommend giving them to a friend or family member, and then re-enacting a proper Oxbridge medicine interview. The questions start off easier, and slowly become more and more tricky, which is similar to how Oxbridge medicine interview scenarios develop.

If you would like to have some mock Oxford and Cambridge medicine interviews with our expert Oxbridge tutors, then feel free to get in touch with us – https://www.medicmind.co.uk/oxbridge-interview-tutors/

Oxford and Cambridge Medicine Interview Scenario 1: Haemoglobin

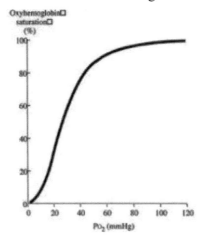

Describe the graph

- As the partial pressure of oxygen increases, so does the haemoglobin saturation.

- Sigmoid shape

Why is the graph this shape?

- Results from changes in the binding ability of haemoglobin as oxygen binds

- Each haemoglobin can bind 4 oxygen molecules, with the 2nd and 3rd molecules being the easiest to bind- this results in the steep gradient in the middle section of the graph

Why is this advantageous for humans?

- The flat upper portion- if the alveolar PO2 falls, the loading of oxygen will be unaffected

- Steep section- assists oxygen diffusion into tissue, allowing tissues to withdraw enough oxygen without big changes in PO2

Draw / Describe the effects of carbon dioxide on the shape of the graph

- Bohr effect

- High carbon dioxide- binds and shift curve to the right enhancing O2 unloading. Helpful in respiring tissues

How might this graph be different in a foetus?

- Fetal haem has a higher affinity for oxygen- right shift

- Important as it allows oxygen to be taken up at lower partial pressures of oxygen from maternal blood to fetal blood

What other factors affect the oxygen carrying capacity of the blood?

- Amount of red blood cells (and therefore the amount of haemoglobin). Can be increased at altitude, where oxygen in the atmosphere is lower
- Oxygen dissolved in the plasma

Oxford and Cambridge Medicine Interview Scenario 2: Vaccines

How do vaccines work?

- Administer antigens in various forms to elicit an immune response and develop memory.
- Production of antibodies (B cells) and T cells
- Formation of memory cells which can mount a faster and more specific immune response upon reinfection
- They protect an individual against the harmful symptoms of infection and prevent that person transmitting the pathogen to someone else (herd immunity)

Can you name any types of vaccine?

- Live attenuated vaccine- weakened form of pathogen
- Inactivated- dead pathogen
- Subunit/polysaccharide- just the antigenic part

What are the risks of live vaccines?

- Revert to virulence- cause disease
- Mutation of pathogen
- Severe reactions

Why are live vaccines more effective?

- Active replication stimulates the immune response more efficiently- more likely to develop long-lasting immunity
- Get both an antibody and T cell response

What types of vaccines do you know are being used for COVID?

- RNA vaccines- use the body's cells to produce the antigen. No risk of reversion to virulence
- Vector vaccine (oxford)- common cold virus with instructions to make COVID proteins

How would you design an ethical study to test how effective a vaccine was?

- Randomised, double blind trial
- Half participants get placebo (What is the importance of a placebo-control?)
- Challenge trials- ethical issue if people get disease and get seriously ill
- Alternative is wait for natural infection and see what % was in placebo group

Can you think of any viruses or other infectious disease that we don't have a vaccine for yet, and suggest why this might be?

- HIV- infects immune cells and kills them. Also rapidly mutations so antigens change

- Malaria- natural infection does not elicit immune protection. Lack of funding as it doesn't affect many higher-income countries.

Oxford and Cambridge Medicine Interview Scenario 3: Antibiotics

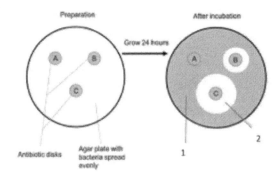

What is the arrow labelled 1 pointing at?

- Bacterial growth

- Agar plate contains the nutrients needed for bacteria to grow at the correct temperatures

What is the arrow labelled 2 pointing at?

- Zone of inhibition (area with no bacterial growth)

Why is there no bacteria growing here?

- Antibiotic is killing the bacteria, by preventing their growth, division and replication

Which of these is the best antibiotic and why?

- C, because it has the largest zone of inhibition, meaning that this bacterial is more susceptible to this type of antibiotic

What makes a successful antibiotic?

- Selective toxicity against bacteria and not host cells

- Target bacterial function that is essential

- Wide therapeutic index (not highly toxic)

- Minimal impacts on host flora

Why is there no zone of inhibition around A?

- Could be a control soaked in saline solution

- Could be a type of bacterial that has developed resistance to the antibiotic and therefore cannot inhibit its growth

What do you understand by the term antimicrobial resistance, and by what mechanisms might a bacteria be resistant?

- Bacteria is no longer susceptible to a particular antibiotic

- Bacterial become resistant via mutations and changes in the genetic material that allow; efflux of the drug, inactivation of the drug e.g. by enzymatic degradation, modification of the protein or process that the drug targets

How can we combat antimicrobial resistance?

- Decrease use of antibiotics e.g. in agriculture

- Use only for bacterial infections

- Make sure patients finish their course of antibiotics

- Use combinations of drugs- more effective

- Develop new antibiotics

10.3 The Day of the Oxbridge Interview

10 On-The-Day Tips for Oxford and Cambridge Medical Interviews

No amount of revision will be enough to get you into Oxbridge if you can't make it bear fruit at the interviews themselves. Here are ten tips for perfecting your interview technique and presenting the best version of yourself on the day.

1. Think out loud

Reminding yourself to think out loud is the best way to avoid the deafening silence that is everyone's worst interview nightmare. Oxbridge dons aren't looking for someone with all the answers – they can teach you those themselves if you get in. In fact, they usually make a point of taking you past the limits of your knowledge in order to see how you grapple with new problems. This is seen as a better indicator of academic potential than your ability to regurgitate known facts.

Thinking out loud will help you when challenged in this way, because you'll be showing them signs of logical thinking and giving them the chance to direct your musings towards an answer.

2. Don't be afraid to give a simple answer

One of the most common reasons candidates stop thinking out loud is that they're afraid to say anything simple or 'obvious'. Wanting to seem as clever as possible is reasonable, but the best way to answer a complex question is by starting with the basics. And what's more, some of the questions you'll face will be seeking simple, even GCSE-level answers; Oxbridge interviewees – particularly those who've put in the most preparation – are often disarmed by this.

3. Answer the question

On a similar note: answer the question that's been put to you each time, avoiding the temptation to show off any in-depth but unrelated knowledge you may have. Going off on tangents is unlikely to impress your interviewers, who will know more about any topic than you do and will interpret such behaviour as failure to understand their questions. Worse still, it wastes valuable time that could come in handy later on for working through the hardest questions that offer more scope for impressing.

4. Help yourself by asking questions

If you're not sure what an interviewer means, feel free to ask for clarification or even for them to repeat themselves. You'll feel less stupid and make a better impression for having a phrase explained than for barking up the wrong tree over several consecutive questions.

5. Don't take things personally

A failing of some candidates is to take the tough questioning of their interviewers personally. If you feel as though an interviewer is nitpicking, deliberately misunderstanding you or offering minimal help as you flounder for answers, chances are that they'll be doing the same to all the other candidates. Remember that this is par for the course and don't be put off.

6. Be personable

One quirk of Oxbridge is that a number of your interviewers are likely to have close dealings with you via the collegiate tutorial (Oxford) or supervision (Cambridge) system. This means they'll be thinking about what you'd be like to teach and meet with on a weekly basis. You shouldn't have to do anything out of the ordinary to do well on this one – just try to be polite and attentive, and walk in with a smile on your face.

7. Expect the unexpected

Unconventional questions are a staple of the Oxbridge interview process, designed to reveal how you think on your feet and apply what you've learnt in unfamiliar ways. Aside from preparing for such questions in the first place (see our article on Oxbridge preparation), you should respond to them with an open mind. Look no further than the material you've revised when concocting a response – they wouldn't ask you something you didn't know enough to answer.

8. Remember who you're up against

It's easy to feel intimidated by your interviewers – brainiacs with years of experience in the field they're asking you about. But remember: you're not trying to outsmart them. In fact, the people you're competing with are the same age as you, at the same stage in their academic studies, and you'll all be subjected to the same interview process. Bearing this in mind should lower the bar you set for yourself and help you relax.

9. Clear your mind beforehand

Cramming immediately before your interview is arguably an even worse idea than cramming for an exam. Oxbridge interviews challenge you to grapple with new concepts and think creatively about familiar ones, all of which is best attempted with a clear head. Use the minutes before an interview to relax and focus on the basics of your interview technique.

10. Wear whatever you're comfortable in

Oxford and Cambridge may be old-fashioned but your interviewers won't expect you to turn up in formal clothing. Anything goes, although dressing too informally could suggest you don't care enough about the interview and overdressing may only make you feel self-conscious and tense. Within sensible limits, you should wear the clothes in which you feel most comfortable.

CHAPTER 11

XI Communication & Roleplay

11.1 Role Play

Most UK medical schools will host at least one role play situation as part of their MMIs. In fact, these stations are becoming increasingly popular even amongst traditional interview setups. This is because role-plays allow interviewers to assess real time communication skills by examining the candidates in scenarios that require empathy, good listening skills and more!

Expert's Advice

Role-play stations often cause the most panic among candidates. Overcoming this is the most important part of performing well in these stations. Remember that your examiners are not looking for oscar-worthy acting performances, nor are they going to judge your medical knowledge. Rather, they are simply looking for basic communication skills that can form the foundation for further training in medical school. By reminding yourself of this fact, you are more likely to remain calm and true to yourself throughout and this is, in fact, the best approach to any MMI role-play station.

There are a wide variety of role-play scenarios that are popular in medical interviews. Therefore, it is nearly impossible to pre-prepare your exact dialogue. If anything, this method should be avoided as for any MMI station, but more so for role-plays. However, below are some global tips to apply to all role-plays to maximize your performance

- **Introduce yourself.** Always introduce your full name and role (typically, medical student or junior doctor) to the person you're speaking to. Additionally, if role-playing a clinical scenario, remember to check the patient's full name and date of birth. Asking them for permission to speak to them will also show empathy and consideration for your "patient", leaving a good impression on examiners.

- **Use eye contact appropriately.** Eye-contact is a wonderful way to show empathy whilst remaining professional. Whilst conversing with friends and family, get into the habit of maintaining eye-contact to ensure that this comes naturally during your MMI.

- **Avoid hand-shakes.** In many professional environments, a hand-shake is considered a neutral and professional introduction. However, this is often not the case in medical scenarios for a multitude of reasons. Therefore, avoid shaking the hand of your examiner or the person with whom you're role-playing.

- **Be aware of facial expressions.** Be conscious of the situation at hand and smile or remain neutral as appropriate. For example, a smile or laugh may help improve rapport in friendly "patient-doctor" conversations. However, be conscious of your facial expressions during more serious conversations.

- **Practice your body language.** Different role-play stations will demand different conversational styles. However, generally speaking, avoid slouching or sitting casually. Avoid touching a patient, even when showing empathy (though, offering a tissue or tea when a patient is upset will often help you score highly). Nodding also shows good listening skills so employ this where appropriate.

- **Start open and then go closed.** Begin by asking open questions to gather maximum information. These are questions that cannot be answered with a 'yes' or 'no'. Examples include "How can I help you today?" or "Can you please tell me more about that?". Once you have gathered more information, proceed to closed questions (i.e.; yes or no or short answer questions) to get more targeted information.
- **Never lie or falsely reassure.** As aforementioned, examiners will not comment on your medical knowledge and so, if you are unsure about something, be honest and avoid lying to appease the actors. Instead, reassure them that you will get an answer from a senior or will signpost them to relevant resources.

A general skeleton to follow for role-play situations will look as follows;

1. **Introduction:** "Hi, I'm [insert name here], your doctor today. Can I please confirm your name and date of birth? Lovely to meet you. Is it okay if we discuss [insert presenting complaint here] today?"
2. **Start with open conversations:** "How are you feeling about this?", "Why do you feel this way?"
3. **ICE:** Explore their ideas, concerns and expectations. Show empathy through non-verbal and verbal communication whilst doing so, for example, by saying "I'm sorry to hear that, that must have been very difficult for you".
4. **Closing and summary:** Ensure you arrange a solution, summarize and thank the patient for their time. "Thank you for speaking to me today. Do you have any questions for me? I will discuss this with my seniors so we can come up with a plan to get everything sorted as soon as possible, we can follow-up in a week's time"

11.2 Data Interpretation

Data interpretation stations are not very common in MMIs. However, some universities do prioritize them quite highly as they are a good way to assess logical and problem-solving skills. Therefore, preparing for them is vital as, if present, it is often an easy station to score highly in.

Data Interpretation stations often involve graphical or tabular data that must be interpreted in order to answer a series of questions. The ability to make logical conclusions from presented data is key. Often, there will be follow-up questions that center around the subject discussed within the data given to you. Therefore, some basic scientific knowledge will be required for these stations. However, revising common A-Level Biology topics will be more than enough and no detailed clinical knowledge will be required.

In navigating data interpretation questions, here are some things to keep in mind.

1. **Understand what the data is for, starting with the axes.** Study the context of the data given, and be sure to comment on the x and y axes of the graph.
2. **Draw on any obvious conclusions.** Often, the data will be presented in a line graph. Comment on any obvious trends in the graph, such as net downward or upward trends.
3. **Multiple graphs.** If you are presented with multiple graphs, comment on them one by one before looking at them together to comment on the ways in which they correlate. For example, you may be presented with one graph commenting on the incidence of diabetes across a decade whilst a second graph may showcase obesity rates across the same decade. Once you have commented on general trends in the individual graphs, comment on whether there is any correlation in diabetes incidence and increasing obesity.
4. **Use real-world or external information when answering questions.** Using the aforementioned example of diabetes and obesity incidences, be sure to draw on experiences from work-experience or school courses to further bolster your answer.
5. **Ask for more data.** Remember that they are looking to examine skills in logical thinking. Therefore, it will showcase very well to comment on the need for more data across a larger population and more time to fully comment on chronic trends.

Some data interpretation stations will also require calculation. This can be calculating the amount of local anesthetic to administer, the cost of treatments and more! You will not require any more than basic A-level chemistry and maths knowledge but being aware of common formulae and rearranging of equations will hold you in good stead.

Expert's Advice

A common formula to be familiar with is that for calculating concentration (for example, of drugs in a solution). This can be calculated using;

Concentration (mmol/ml) = amount (mmol)/volume (ml)

Finally, knowing basic conversions on the back of your hand will help you save time and improve your confidence in data interpretation and calculations stations.

Unit 1	Unit 2
1 Milligram	1000 Micrograms
1 Gram	1000 Milligrams 1000000 Micrograms
1 Kilogram	1000 Grams 1000000 Milligrams 1000000000 Micrograms

Mock Station #1:

To confirm diabetes, a person will normally take a glucose tolerance test in a hospital. Patients do not eat for 12 hours before the test. This gets their blood glucose to its lowest. They are then given a drink containing 75g of glucose and their blood glucose level is monitored over the next 2 hours. The graph for a healthy versus a diabetic patient is shown below.

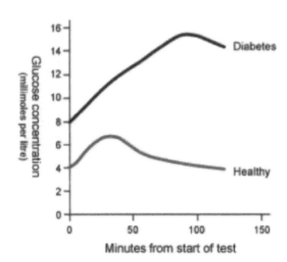

1. Describe the trend shown.
2. Explain the mechanism which causes glucose levels to fall in the healthy patient.
3. Explain the mechanism of Type 1 diabetes and how it explains the trend shown for the diabetic patient.
4. Why does the patient have to fast prior to the glucose tolerance test?

Mock Answer:

"These graphs show the trends in glucose concentration over roughly 120 minutes, or 2 hours, following the consumption of the glucose drink in a healthy versus a diabetic patient. On the x-axis, we can see the blood glucose concentration whilst the y-axis shows the time. The blue line on the graph indicates that blood glucose levels rise for a longer period of time, roughly 100 minutes, before it starts to fall in a diabetic whilst the pink line shows that in a healthy patient, blood glucose levels reach its peak in roughly half a hour before falling and remaining steady for the remainder of the shown duration. Additionally, diabetics have a higher starting glucose, at 8 mmols/l than in healthy patients who begin with half the glucose level.

In a healthy patient, the drop in glucose levels occurs due to insulin secretion from the pancreas which causes conversion of free glucose to glycogen for storage in the liver. This removes glucose from the blood, causing levels to fall. However, in a type 1 diabetic, there is autoimmune destruction of the insulin producing cells in the pancreas. This causes reduced and slower insulin production thereby lending a lower drop in glucose following consumption of food.

To answer the final question, patients must fast prior to a glucose tolerance test as their blood glucose must reach its lowest point. This prevents previously consumed food from interfering with the glucose levels lending more reliability to the test."

If time permits, candidates may also draw upon any experience during their volunteering or clinical rotations or school courses that have focussed on the pathophysiology or management of diabetes to further bolster their answer.

11.3 Video and Picture Stations

Video and picture stations is a misnomer. These are not individual stations but rather refer to the use of visual aids in a variety of stations, including role-play or communication stations.

If asked to describe a picture, structure your response such that you start big before zooming in. Comment on the context of the image and its larger elements before noticing finer details. These stations will often focus on follow-up questions that rely on an understanding of various basic science and healthcare concepts. Once again, knowledge is not being examined as much as communication and interpretation skills are.

Mock Station #1

Describe this image. How do you think healthcare might be different here?

Mock Answer:

"This picture shows a small township within what looks like a lush field on a sunny day. The township itself appears to be quite remote, however, this cannot be deduced from this photo alone. It appears to be a collection of small buildings, presumably a relatively small, close knit community that thrives on agricultural or farming practices given the location and surrounding land.

With regards to healthcare, these communities pose a unique challenge to care provision. Firstly, there are multiple diagnoses that may be more common in these communities, such as farming-related trauma calls or infectious diseases that doctors must be familiar with. Furthermore, WHO has noted disparities in health outcomes with higher mortality and reduced life expectancy in rural or remote areas, like the one pictured. So, care provision must be tailored to this. Another challenge might be the recruitment and retention of staff in such areas as well as continued professional development opportunities, which are often confined to more urban areas. This might mean delayed development of new and improved care provision in such areas, thereby causing poorer outcomes. Social care and public health awareness may also prove challenging in these environments. However, I believe that medical students must be equipped to care for people in these communities during medical school to better equip future workforces to cater to a wide range of the population."

If time permits, candidates are also encouraged to allude to any remote working or volunteering opportunities that they have done or any rural medicine modules available at the medical school where they are interviewing as these elements can improve station scores.

11.4 Group Tasks

Sometimes known as Problem Based Learning (PBL) stations, these are used to assess candidates in their ability to work together as a team, take on leadership roles and communicate effectively towards a common goal. Whilst the PBL method of teaching is increasingly popular at British medical schools, these stations may be employed by any medical school as teamwork and leadership are core values for any doctor and so, are important to assess.

PBL interview stations can include a wide array of tasks and so, it is more important to focus on a few general rules to follow as opposed to preparing for a specific group task. These include;

1. **Do not speak over anyone.** You need to highlight impressive communication skills, and this includes active listening and politeness. Do not interrupt other candidates and only make your point within the context of what has already been said when there is a break in conversation. When others are speaking, tilt your body towards them, nod and listen intently to showcase good listening skills.

2. **Analyse the given scenario.** Assess what the scenario represents, any problems it brings to light and the various stakeholders that are affected by the scenario. Thinking out loud will help bring these topics forward to the group, opening up the floor for others' opinions and showcasing yourself as a natural leader in the conversation.

3. **Encourage others to speak.** A common mistake candidates make in these stations is to speak as much as possible to ensure that their opinion is heard. However, it is well known that any one individual taking over a meeting is often not well-received. Open the floor for other discussions and allow your peers to speak. Asking them to comment on arguments you have brought up shows that you are a keen collaborator and work well within any team.

4. **Engage in a natural manner.** If appropriate, make tasteful jokes, be encouraging of your peers and interact in a friendly, yet confident manner. It is helpful to think of these stations as a conversation amongst friends, as opposed to a debate; the latter often brings out a more argumentative side which must be avoided to score highly in this station.

5. **Be conscious of your body language.** Remain confident, maintain eye contact and smile where appropriate. Use your hands or nod your head to acknowledge conversation and avoid slouching or shrugging during the station.

CHAPTER 12

XII Extra MMI Stations

Motivation for Medicine

MMI Station: Which Specialty? / PS

Station Brief: What is the most important part of your personal statement and why? The interviewer will now ask you a series of questions on your personal statement.

Notes for Interviewer

- Pick out any work experience they've done and ask about what they may want to specialise in
- Pick out any books / research, and ask why they found it interesting

Good answer A good answer may include:

- **e.g. Pick out a particular achievement.** You could pick out an extracurricular or academic achievement you talked about. It could be your most important because it is special to you and you are proud of it.
- **e.g. Work experience paragraph**. It could be that your work experience really drove you towards medicine, so discussing this could have been really important for you.
- **Knowing your PS inside out.** It is so important to be ready for this kind of question. You should be comfortable to talk about whichever part they pick out.
- **Expand on your PS.** Go beyond what is written in your PS. If they ask about a work experience placement, don't list the same points you wrote down. Talk about different things you saw.

Poor answer A poor answer may include:

- **Picking several parts.** The question asks for the most important part, not multiple parts.
- **Not explaining importance.** Don't just explain that part of your personal statement. You need to go beyond whats written - why was it so, so important for you?

MMI Station: Wider Reading

Station Brief: Discuss an article you have read recently relating to medicine.

- Why did you find it interesting?
- What is your opinion?
- How would you find out more about it?

Good answer A good answer may include:

- **Recent article.** An interesting article which is relatively recent (e.g. within the past 6 months)
- **Linking it to your personal experience.** e.g. work experience and what you saw in a

hospital
- **Giving an opinion**. Giving your own opinion rather than just stating what the article said.

Poor answer A poor answer may include:

- **Simplistic or old article**. e.g. an article about using sweets in paediatric wards.
- **Just stating the article**. Not giving an opinion, and instead just explaining what the article said.
- **Making it up!** Some students have done no reading or preparation, so try to lie - and its obvious!

Golden Tip: During stage 1 of our programme, you would have touched upon this particular question. So in your handbook you should have an article ready, and ideally link it to some extra research you have done (or will do). Saying 'this article inspired me to give a talk at my school during lunch time on the topic' sounds very proactive! It takes 1 hour to prepare a talk, and it could be a 15 minute talk in front of 5 people at lunch time.

MMI Station: Speaking to a patient

Station Brief: A 83 year old man, Vishnu is living in a nursing home. He has late-stage Alzheimer's disease, and has been struggling with his memory and finds it hard to take care of himself.

Speak to Vishnu about his experiences inside the care home, and ask him about advice he would give to doctors working in a nursing home and advice he would give to other patients who were about to move into the nursing home.

Good answer A good answer may include:

- You need to show clear empathy in this scenario, and display that you have insight into a career in medicine by showing this.

- A good way of doing this is by asking her how this experience has affected her.

- You as a doctor would review this decision if there was any change in his condition.

Poor answer A poor answer may include:

- Being patronising, and saying things like 'I can't imagine what it must be like for you'.
- Asking her about a distressing situation.
- Fixating on anything negative.
- Just focusing on the first part of the question and not both parts.

Examiner's Tip: Use body language to your advantage here. Things like nodding and good eye contact will show the examiner that you have motivation to help patients like Margaret in the future. Avoid sitting in a closed   position   away   from   the   actor.

MMI Station: Skills required in Medicine

Station Brief: The examiner will be asking you the following questions:

1. Tell me about your communication skills.

2. Would you say communication is more important than academic/scientific ability or would you say it is less important?

3. Can you give me an example of when you've worked in a team, when you've been in a stressful situation and how you've managed that.

4. What is the importance of having the continuity of care, such as in GP practices?

Good answer A good answer may include:

- Give very concise answers, and made sure that they weren't waffling

- Using the STARR template with sufficient examples

- Being reflective and considering what skills the interviewers are looking for.

- Linking back to medicine.

Poor answer A poor answer may include:

- Not respond directly to the question and waffling

- Sounding overly rehearsed and being unnatural in your response.

- Going straight into the question without thinking about what to say.

- Being generic and vague.

Examiner's Tip: Ensure you are concise in your answers. What can often happen is that candidates get carried away with one question, forgetting that a station consists of up to 4-5 questions.

MMI Station: Work Experience

Station Brief: This station is focused on your reflections from work experience. **Why did you do work experience?** (Part 1 of 2)

Good answer A good answer may include:

- **To learn more about medicine.** You wanted to see medicine first-hand to help you decide if this was the career for you.

- **Out of interest.** You have always been passionate about hospitals, so you were keen to see things first hand.

- **To see the different sectors of medicine**. You wanted to see the differences between medicine in a GP practice, A&E, a surgery and a hospital specialty ward.

Poor answer A poor answer may include:

- **Because you had to.** Don't say you did work experience because it was compulsory. You want to come across as keen and interested in medicine.

- **To improve your UCAS application.** e.g. 'I tried really hard to do work experience abroad to improve my UCAS application. This is due to my motivation to get in and study medicine'.

Station Brief: This station is focused on your reflections from work experience. **What did you do and learn in your work experience? Tell me as much as possible from your placements in with a GP, a consultant, a surgeon, a nurse or another healthcare professional. You can talk about one or multiple.** (Part 2 of 2)

Good answer A good answer may include:

- **Teamwork -** between surgeons, nurses, anaesthetists, physiotherapists.

- **Post-Operative Care -** continuity of care for patients.

- **Clinics -** enjoyed shadowing doctor clinics with patients to follow up on their surgery.

Poor answer A poor answer may include:

- **Taking a History -** interesting to see the unique approach of each doctor to take a history and diagnose a patient.

- **Holistic Approach -** interesting to see how doctors balanced the need to be friendly and caring, and the need to be time efficient.

- **Ward Rounds -** these were great, as I saw so many different patients in a short time.

MMI Station: Rural Medicine

Station Brief: What do you know about rural medicine? Why is that important at our university? What can you bring to our university? Why did you choose St Andrew's?

Good answer A good answer may include:

- **New facilities.** The university recently went through a refurbishment, so the campus is modern and of high quality.

- **Teaching   style.**   Traditional   learning   with   predominantly   lectures.

- **Discussion scenarios.** Alongside traditional lectures, there are problem based discussion scenarios, giving you a variety of learning styles.

Poor answer A poor answer may include:

- **Focusing on generic things.** Some students may discuss the 'great teaching quality' and 'fantastic resources' without being specific (e.g. by quoting the recent refurbishment).

- **Focusing on menial things.** Some students may talk too much about casual things. Societies are good to mention, but don't spend your whole answer on that. And don't talk about the nightlife as a big incentive for going to St Andrew's!

- **Lacking a balance.** Focusing too much on either the city or the university, rather than covering both points in the time you have.

Work Experience

MMI Station: Online GPs

Station Brief: Read this news article for 2 minutes, and then discuss the pros and cons of this new technology

A 24-hour service has been launched for NHS patients, offering GP consultations via video link on smartphones. Patients will be able to check their symptoms through the mobile app and then have video consultations within two hours of booking. The new free service has been launched by a group of London GPs and the online healthcare provider Babylon. Patients joining will leave their existing practice, with their records transferred to a group of five central London surgeries.

Dr Mobasher Butt, said; "We've benefited from this kind of technology in so many different aspects of our lives, whether that be shopping or banking, and it's really time that we were able to do that in healthcare for NHS patients."

Jane Barnacle, director of patients and information at NHS England London, said GP practices were right to carefully test innovative new technologies that could improve free NHS services for their patients while also freeing up staff time.

Pros of the Technology

Good answer A good answer may include:

- Increased access to care (24h) - more patients seen.

- In line with modern technology and trends - e.g. used for e-learning in education.

- Saves time and therefore money.

Poor answer A poor answer may include:

- It is cool to have a doctor from a phone.

- Can be a stepping stone to integration into things like Snapchat and Instagram.

- You can call up a GP even for minor problems.

Examiner's Tip - Try to link in your own work experience. If you have seen a GP practice struggle with bookings, then you can really go the extra mile - e.g. "Whilst shadowing a GP, I saw the struggle of managing the huge number of patients, so this type of service could really help to reduce physical in-person demand."

Cons of the Technology

Good answer A good answer may include:

- Lack of personal touch.

- Misdiagnosis as the patient cannot be examined.

- Likely to be referred to GP regardless.

- Doctors may spend more time on this and less practicing.

- Patient confidentiality and data handling.

Poor answer A poor answer may include:

- Will take up more staff time.

- It's not good to use any technology in medicine.

- Some people may not like mobile phones.

- Medicine is different to banking or shopping.

- GP services don't have any problems

MMI Station: Work Experience

Station Brief: Why did you do work experience? From your work experience, what did you observe that underpinned your interest for Medicine? Was there any lesson or observation which you feel stuck out the most? Why did it seem so important?

Good answer A good answer may include:

- **Structured approach.** STARR method is useful. Speak in a logical and structured method - avoid being too long-winded, but give enough detail to set the scene.

- **Discuss personal research.** e.g. 'I saw a patient with Chronic Kidney Disease, and it inspired me to do my own personal research. To raise awareness, I gave a talk at my school during a lunch time'. It takes 60 minutes to do some research and prepare a short talk, and the talk could be to 5 friends - do it!

Poor answer A poor answer may include:

- **Not picking a specific patient.** Students have a tendency to talk too generically about patients in general, without picking a specific patient.

- **Not knowing much about the condition.** This question is focusing on the condition that the patient has as well as the patient as a person. It won't look good if you haven't done your research about the patient's condition and treatment.

- **Lying.** If you try to lie about a patient, it could get found out. You may say something which isn't correct for a certain condition and this will look odd.

MMI Station: Qualities of Doctors

Station Brief: Part 1 of 2

1. What are important qualities of a doctor? Please discuss these.
    - **Teamwork** is important as a doctor when you work in multidisciplinary teams, such as in surgery where you work with anaesthetists, nurses and other clinicians
    - **Leadership** is important as a doctor as you need to manage multidisciplinary teams, and show leadership to both the patient and colleagues.
    - **Communication** is essential to build a doctor patient relationship.
    - **Organisation** is key for managing time with tasks
    - **Other qualities** include empathy, compassion, strong scientific knowledge, manual dexterity, calmness, organisation and more.

2. What do you know about the NHS values and can you name any?

    - **Link to GMC guidelines.** It is useful to link in the GMC guidelines, as we discussed in station 1 of this mock.

    - **Care for patients.** Patients are at the focus of the NHS, and it is important that they are always treated fairly, with integrity and confidentiality maintained.

    - **Keeping up to date.** The NHS strives to keep up to date with modern science and evolve as better treatments are discovered.

    - **Free at the point of care.** The NHS is free at the point of care, and this is one of its most unique and important features.

3. What is more important as a doctor? Being intelligent or having empathy?

Intelligent

- **Scientific knowledge.** It is important to be intelligent to be able to learn and understand the high-level science in medicine.

- **Social intelligence.** As a doctor you are involved in many careful and delicate situations, so you need good social awareness and intelligence.

- **Constant learning.** Medicine is always evolving, so you need a high level of intelligence to constantly improve and learn.

Empathy

- **Speaking to patients.** It is essential to speak to patients in a calming and comfortable way. Without this, the patient might not open up to you, and you may struggle to find a diagnosis regardless of your intelligence.

- **Medicine is a holistic art**. Medicine is more than a science - it is also an art. And the need to be caring and communicate well is evident.

4. What is the difference between empathy and sympathy?

- **Empathy is understanding how someone feels**. Empathy is the ability to be able to actually understand what someone is feeling. For example, if you have been through a similar situation to a patient, you are more able to feel empathy. Although even if you haven't been through the situation, you can feel empathy.

- **Empathy is like putting yourself in someone's shoes**. A good term to use is 'putting yourself in someone's shoes'

- **Sympathy is feeling sorry for someone**. Sympathy is the act of feeling sorry for someone's situation. However, you may not be able to actually understand what they are going through.

Station Brief: Part 2 of 2

Steph Houghton is a fantastic leader and captain of England Women's Football Team. What kind of qualities would a football captain ideally have? How can these same skills be applied in medicine for the lead consultant in a multidisciplinary team?

Football Captain

- **Approachable -** needs to be approachable and a good listener. If any player has an issue, or is low on morale, they should feel comfortable coming to the captain

- **Motivator -** should be able to motivate others, e.g. in the team talk

- **Organisation -** needs to be organised, and know his team well. He is responsible for each person.

- **Hard worker -** the leader needs to be one of the hardest working. They need to lead by example.

- **Authoritative -** as well as listening to others, the leader needs to be decisive and show authority. He / she needs to be respected.

Multidisciplinary Team Leader

- **Approachable** - medicine can be stressful, so the leader of a MDT needs to be approachable for all healthcare specialists in their team.

- **Motivator** - should be able to motivate the team and patients

- **Organisation** - needs to be organised as they have the ultimate responsibility for patients

- **Hard worker** - the lead doctor has many team members to manage, so they need to work hard

- **Authoritative** - decisions in medicine can often be subjective. Doctors may disagree, so a decisive leader is needed.

Medical Ethics

MMI Station: Consent and Capacity

Station Brief: Q1/3 What do you understand about the phrase 'informed consent?' Why is it important to make sure patients are providing informed consent?

Good answer A good answer may include:

- **Define consent.** The patient agrees to and allows a specific action to be taken (procedure, medication, etc.)

- **Define informed.** Patients must understand the particular procedure prior to providing consent, including what is involved, why it is being done, and potential side effects. This ensures competence.

- **Discuss importance**. Understanding that patients need to be aware of what specifically they are consenting to, and the implications.

- **Speak about autonomy.** If patients are not providing informed consent, this means they lose a great level of autonomy. Perhaps explore medical paternalism.

Poor answer A poor answer may include:

- **Having a poor understanding**. Not understanding what informed consent means, or not discussing the 'informed' aspect of informed consent.

- **Not mentioning autonomy**. Failing to mention that patients must provide consent otherwise medical staff are ignoring their autonomy.

- **Poor exploration of ethics.** Understanding what informed consent is but not connecting it to the ethical issues at hand (acting in the best interest of the patient while respecting autonomy).

Q2/3 What are some of the issues raised if medical staff inappropriately obtain informed consent? When might a patient not provide informed consent?

Good answer A good answer may include:

- **Ethical considerations**. Failure to respect patient autonomy directly negates one of the pillars of medical ethics. This is a serious offence.

- **Poor rapport**. If medical staff do procedures without asking consent, the patient may feel powerless. This does not establish a healthy relationship with the patient.

- **Health implications.** Perhaps the patient has a medically-relevant reason for not consenting to a procedure (side effects) and this helps patients take their health into their own hands.

- **Sets a poor example.** Medicine has come a long way since its initial paternalistic approach. Inappropriately obtaining consent makes medicine regress to lower standards.

Poor answer A poor answer may include:

- **One-sided approach.** Discusses only the medical impact or the ethical impact.

- **Does not explore autonomy.** May mention autonomy but does not explore what patient autonomy does for the patient with regards to their input in their own disease management.

- **Fails to mention doctor-patient relationship.** Lack of exploration as to why this is important and how to strengthen it.

- **Does not recognise pattern.** Does not mention that assuming consent or assuming a patient is 'informed' becomes an unhealthy pattern of behaviour.

Q3/3 Are there any instances in which medical staff may proceed with a particular action without obtaining informed consent?

Good answer A good answer may include:

- **If the patient is unconscious.** The patient would be unable to provide consent, so family/carers should be consulted.

- **If the patient does not consent.** This would happen if they do not want the procedure done, for many reasons.

- **When a patient is not competent.** Patients unable to understand the procedure either due to young age or cognitive impairment cannot provide informed consent.

- **Life-changing and time-sensitive procedures.** For certain procedures (ex. CPR, stopping a major bleed), time is of the essence and the procedure can continue. Be mindful of patients who do not want to be resuscitated.

Poor answer A poor answer may include:

- **No ideas of potential scenarios.** No thoughts about times in which a patient may not or be unable to provide informed consent.

- **Too focused on one scenario.** Efforts are not made to consider a range of scenarios in which consent may not be given.

- **Unaware of the law.** Medical staff are allowed to perform some life-saving procedures if a patient is unable to provide consent at the time.

Conclusion / Summary

- Everything in medicine needs consent from a patient who has capacity

- A patient over 16 is implied to have capacity, unless proven otherwise

- A patient under 16 can have capacity if they are Gillick competent

- If a patient is unconscious or unable to give consent, we use any Advanced Directives, or speak to an appointed Lasting Power of Attorney. If these aren't present, we act in the patients best interests.

- This topic is very technical! You probably don't need to know terms such as Advanced Directives or LPA, however just understand the core principles.

MMI Station: Confidentiality

Station Brief: Please watch this video and comment on the behaviour exhibited by the medical student:

https://www.youtube.com/watch?v=rkcDOQZ15FQ&feature=emb_title&ab_channel=GeneralMedicalCouncil

Good answer A good answer may include:

- **Identify the issue.** State that the student is breaching confidentiality.

- **Explain how.** Detail that she provides patient's name, diagnosis, etc.

- **Discuss the environment.** She is speaking about the patient in an open, public space where others can overhear, in addition to the person she is speaking to.

- **Confidentiality.** Discuss why patient confidentiality is in place and how this breaches that.

- **Reference GMC guidelines.** Cite GMC guidelines on patient confidentiality.

Poor answer A poor answer may include:

- **Not mentioning confidentiality.** Either not using the word 'confidentiality' or not explaining why confidentiality is important.

- **Not mentioning specifics.** Not stating how confidentiality was breached by referencing particular   aspects   of   the   video.

- **Not discussing the environment.** Identifying that she is disclosing confidential information over the phone, but not discussing the public environment she is in.

- **Condoning her behaviour.** Saying that she is just discussing information with a colleague.

What are some instances in which patient information can be disclosed?

Multi-disciplinary team. Information regarding a patient's care may be discussed with other members of the multi-disciplinary i.e. nurses, occupational therapists, etc. in order to provide the best standard of care.

- **Referrals.** Patient information can be passed along from primary care to secondary care if patients need to be referred to a specialist for a particular complaint.

- **Harm.** If the patient's condition puts themself or other parties at harm, relevant information can be disclosed to the relevant parties.

- **Family/carer if patient is not competent.** For children who are young or adults who are not competent, information can be shared so that medical decisions, etc. can be made.

- **All with patient's consent.** Before sharing patient information, even in the above cases, consent should be obtained from the patient (is it okay if I pass along this information to X for this particular purpose?)

- **All in the appropriate environment.** Speaking about patient information should only be done in confidential spaces in clinical environments, never over social media or other insecure IT systems.

MMI Station:

Station Brief: You are part of the committee responsible for deciding the order of patients on a waiting list for a new liver. Currently, you are discussing three patients, aged 23, 40, and 77 who are all in need of a new liver. What factors are important in making your decision?

Good answer A good answer may include:

- **Age.** Younger patients would generally live longer if given the liver transplant, meaning more QALYs (Quality Adjusted Life Years) will be saved.

- **Biological match.** Are the patients biological matches for the liver, including HLA? Is the size of the liver appropriate for the size of the patient?

- **Alcoholism status.** Is there a risk of alcoholism? If so, will there eventually be a need for another liver if they revert?

- **Urgency.**   Consider   the   urgency   of   need   for   the   liver   transplant.

- **Contribution to society/others.** Do the patients have dependents? Are they gainfully employed?

Poor answer A poor answer may include:

- **Not considering enough factors.** Despite the fact that age is mentioned in the brief, speaking exclusively about age and not mentioning other factors.

- **Being judgmental.** Saying that if the liver transplant was needed due to self-inflicted disease, the patient does not deserve the liver.

- **Making an immediate decision.** Not discussing with your fellow committee members the multiple factors involved that make this a difficult decision.

MMI Station: Organ Donation

Station Brief: Until recently, the entire UK is operated on an opt-in system, whereby by default option is no donation. Discuss opt-in organ donation schemes, and other methods to increase donations of organs in the UK

Pros of Opt-Out

- **More donations** there will be more donations, and therefore more lives saved. This supports the ethical pillar of beneficence.

- **Saves administration** there will be less donors lost because of the administration effort required to donate.

- **Psychological push** people are more likely to donate if already opted in by default.

- **Non maleficence** - no harm is caused to the patient if an organ is extracted after death

Cons of Opt-Out

- **Autonomy** - people may not know they have been opted in by default, and therefore can lose control over their autonomy for their organs. In Wales, many people did not know about the change to an opt-out system.

- **Psychological effects -** it puts pressure on an individual and the altruistic nature of donating an organ is decreased.

- However, the above could be fixed by having a simple, clear method for people to opt out if they so wish.

MMI Station: Specialties

Station Brief: Multidisciplinary teams in medicine involve professionals with different roles. Could you give me an example of a multidisciplinary team which you have seen in your work experience or read about? **Discuss how they worked together. (Part 1 of 2)**

Each member of a multidisciplinary team had their individual, specific career path. What **is the specific training and timescale required of becoming a fully qualified GP? (Part 2 of 2)**

e.g. Surgical Team

- The surgeon performs the operation, requiring intricate manual dexterity and composure.

- The anaesthetist administers the initial anaesthetic, and then has to monitor the patient during surgery

- The nurse is responsible for day-to-day care of the patient in the days preceding and following surgery.

- The physiotherapist and occupational therapist may work with the patient to guide them along post-operative recovery.

Good answer A good answer may include:

- **Explain the role of teamwork.** Discuss how each team member plays a unique role, and how the different specialists link together to make a good team.

- **Mention MDT meetings.** Multidisciplinary teams often have MDT meetings, where they discuss patient cases. It would be useful to mention these in your answer.

MMI Station: Conduct of Medical Students

Station Brief: As an SGUL medical student, it is important to obey our set code of conduct. In this station, the interviewer will ask you a few questions about the role of healthcare students and professionals.

Why is it important for medical students and doctors to remain professional? (Part 1 of 3)

Good answer A good answer may include:

- **To ensure patient trust.** Patients will not trust doctors if they do not act professionally. For example, if a patient is undergoing surgery, they will feel more nervous and anxious if their surgeon is joking around and acting childishly on the ward

- **To prevent patients with-holding information.** If doctors are not professional, patients might hold back information, which would make diagnosis more difficult.

- **To prevent bad press.** The NHS often receives bad press due to struggles to meet targets, so adding more pressure wouldn't be good. Stories of doctors doing silly things can really heap pressure on the NHS, and affect the public perception of doctors.

Station Brief: As an Aberdeen medical student, it is important to obey our set code of conduct. In this station, the interviewer will ask you a few questions about the role of healthcare students and professionals.

What is the importance of being ethical as a doctor? (Part 2 of 3)

Good answer A good answer may include:

- **To be fair to patients.** If you are unethical, it is not fair on patients. You have to ensure that you do everything possible to treat patients and help improve their health in a fair manner.

- **To prevent discrimination.** It is essential to be non-biased with patients. For example, if a smoker walks in with lung cancer, you shouldn't put less effort in because their condition is self-inflicted.

- **To maintain confidentiality.** A key part of ethics is confidentiality. If this is not kept, patients will stop trusting their doctor, and this will make diagnosis and patient management much more difficult.

Examiner's Tip. If Patient A trusted their doctor, they might admit that they smoke 10 cigarettes a day, take cocaine daily, drink alcohol 3x per week and eat lots of take outs. If Patient A didn't trust their doctor, they might only mention the take outs. This would make diagnosis, management and treatment much harder!

Station Brief: As an Aberdeen medical student, it is important to obey our set code of conduct. In this station, the interviewer will ask you a few questions about the role of healthcare students and professionals.

What are the main qualities of a doctor and why are they important? (Part 3 of 3)

Good answer A good answer may include:

- **Teamwork** is important as a doctor when you work in multidisciplinary teams, such as in surgery where you work with anaesthetists, nurses and other clinicians .

- **Leadership** is important as a doctor as you need to manage multidisciplinary teams, and show leadership to both the patient and colleagues.

- **Communication** is essential to build a doctor patient relationship.

- **Organisation** is key for managing time with tasks.

- **Other** qualities include empathy, compassion, strong scientific knowledge, manual dexterity, calmness, organisation and more.

Examiner's Tip. For this question, it is essential to link the skill to your work experience. If you just say that 'teamwork is important', you won't score highly. You need to explain why it is important for doctors, and using your work experience is useful!

MMI Station: Social Media

Station Brief: You are on your gastroenterology rotation and you are on your lunch break. You accidentally glance at your consultant's Twitter page, and they have sent a series of racist tweets about a patient. The consultant has not named the patient in their tweet. **Tell me about the impact that social media can have on medical care? (Part 1 of 3)**

You are on your gastroenterology rotation and you are on your lunch break. You accidentally glance at your consultant's Twitter page, and they have sent a series of racist tweets about a patient. The consultant has not named the patient in their tweet. **How would you advise a doctor who has been added by a patient on facebook? (Part 2 of 3)**

You are on your gastroenterology rotation and you are on your lunch break. You accidentally glance at your consultant's Twitter page, and they have sent a series of racist tweets about a patient. The consultant has not named the patient in their tweet. **Are there any particular issues with the use of social media by medical students? (Part 3 of 3)**

MMI Station: Misconduct of Medical Students

Station Brief: You are the dean of the medical school. One of your lecturer informs you that a group of 10 students came to the lecture intoxicated (drunk). **What should you do in this situation? What ethical issues does this raise? (Part 1 of 3)**

Good answer A good answer may include:

- **Investigate first.** Find out more information on which students, what time of day, how intoxicated they were, and how they were behaving.

- **Arrange a meeting.** Arrange to meet the students to find out what happened, and why they were drinking.

- **Severe punishment.** If found guilty, ensure you adequately punish them to make sure a similar situation doesn't arise in the future.

Poor answer A poor answer may include:

- **Jumping to conclusions.** Don't jump to a conclusion and hand out punishments without knowing the full story?

- **Too light a punishment.** Just a telling off is not sufficient, as this is a very serious situation.

You are the dean of the medical school. One of your lecturer informs you that a group of 10 students came to the lecture intoxicated (drunk). What should you do in this situation? What ethical issues does this raise? **What if you were a medical student in this scenario, and this was one of your friends? How should you approach the situation then? (Part 2 of 3)**

Good answer A good answer may include:

- **Tell them off.** Despite them being your friend, you need to tell them off as this behaviour is not appropriate.

- **Potentially report them.** If you warn them severely, then that may be sufficient. If they do it again, then you should 100% report it.

Poor answer A poor answer may include:

- **Letting them off easy.** In reality, if this was your friend, you'd tell them off lightly but may not escalate it further. However, in the interview you cannot be too honest - you have to act 100% responsibly and do what you 'should' do as a perfect medical student.

- **Escalating it too high.** In some situations, you want to speak to the person, and only escalate it if it is a repeat offence. This is quite a serious case, but you wouldn't immediately escalate it without finding out further information.

Who is the regulatory board that manages the conduct of doctors in the UK? (Part 3 of 3)

Good answer A good answer may include:

- **General Medical Council (GMC).** Explain that they are the regulatory board.

- **'Fitness to Practice'.** Explain that doctors or medical students can receive fitness to practice warnings for bad behaviour.

MMI Station: Being a Team Member

Station Brief: You are the team leader in a group session and you find out that in your team one person has been bullying the other person. The person being bullied is afraid to report this because of the consequences.

What would you do in this scenario? (Part 1 of 2)

Good   answer   A   good   answer   may   include:

- **Speak to the person being bullied.** It is important to reach out to the person who is being bullied to try to understand their fears.

- **Do not break the news to the team.** The person being bullied is clearly worried about repercussions of telling anyone. So it is better to speak to the bullied person first, before blurting anything out in a team meeting.

Poor answer A poor answer may include:

- **Jumping to conclusions.** Don't jump to a conclusion and hand out punishments without knowing the full story? Bullying can range from being slightly rude to someone, to physical bullying. You need to quantify the bullying and then act appropriately.

- **Too light a punishment.** Just a telling off is not sufficient, as this is a very serious situation.

You are the team leader in a group session and you find out that in your team one person has been bullying the other person. The person being bullied is afraid to report this because of the consequences.

There is also another member of your team who is not performing well and putting effort in. What should you do in this scenario? (Part 2 of 2)

Good answer A good answer may include:

- **Speak to that team member.** Have a casual chat with that team member individually. Reach out - find out what is going on in their personal life to search for deeper problems. Also ask about how they are finding the work - is it a case of them not putting effort, or them struggling with the difficulty of the work?

- **Gain a peer assessment.** It may be useful to speak to other team members to gain a peer assessment of their colleagues. This will enable you to better understand the team.

Poor answer A poor answer may include:

- **Jumping to conclusions.** Don't jump to the conclusion that this team member is being lazy. He could have some family issues, or may be struggling with the work. It is important to speak to the team member 1-to-1.

- **Put pressure and pile work on the team member.** It is better to speak to the person in question before piling work on them. If they are struggling, this will only make the situation worse and could dampen his morale.

MMI Station: Confidentiality

Station Brief: A patient diagnosed with HIV reveals to their GP that they have not disclosed this information to their partner. Discuss the ethical issues involved.

Good answer A good answer may include:

- **The doctor should encourage the patient to tell their partner.** The doctor should encourage the patient to tell their partner.

- **You have to break confidentiality if she refuses to tell her partner.** Confidentiality must be broken if the patient is sexually active and refuses to tell their partner.

- **The doctor needs to explain the risks of HIV.** Doctor has to fully inform the patient of the risk associated with HIV.

MMI Station: GMC and Confidentiality

Station Brief: What can you tell me about the General Medical Council's code of conduct for doctors? **(Part 1 of 4)**

Good answer A good answer may include:

- Knowledge, Skills and Performance. This section is about providing a good standard of care, remaining up to date with knowledge and make the care of the patient your first concern!

- Safety and Quality. This section is about taking action when a patient's safety is at risk.

- Communication, Partnership, Teamwork. This section is about treating patients as individuals, maintaining confidentiality and to respect patients.

- Maintaining Trust. This section tells you not to discriminate with patients or abuse their trust. You should act with integrity.

Why is patient confidentiality important? **(Part 2 of 4)**

Good answer A good answer may include:

- It builds the doctor-patient relationship. Patients need to have trust in their doctor, and if there was no confidentiality they may hide details that might be vital to a diagnosis, or they may not even see a doctor if they were ashamed about a disease (e.g. STI)

- Confidentiality is a human right- respect for patient's autonomy.

- Stops exploitation. Prevents exploitation of data (e.g. by insurance companies)

- Improves public confidence in healthcare. This leads to patients being more open and generally trusting doctors a lot.

Do you think it might ever be appropriate to breach a patient's confidentiality? Can you give any examples?   **(Part   3   of   4)**

Good answer A good answer may include:

Yes, in certain situations:

- When there is a risk to a third party (e.g. STI)

- Report road crime to police (Road traffic act).

- When sharing information with other HC professional

Examiner's Tip. Learn these three examples off by heart. Some situations can be subjective - e.g. if a patient is having suicidal thoughts, you may consider breaking confidentiality depending on the situation.

While working at your Saturday job in a shop you find that one of your colleagues has arrived at work smelling of alcohol. They appear to be intoxicated, and you know that they drove to work. What actions would you take? **(Part 4 of 4)**

Good answer A good answer may include:

- **Ease in the conversation.** Try to ease in calmly by asking how they are first. Ask them questions about what they've been doing recently. Look for signs such as lies and slurring of speech.

- **Send them home via public transport.** Tell the colleague it would be better if they take the day off and that they should go home, sober up and have a conversation in the evening somewhere more privately.

- **Address the driving issue.** The alcohol is an issue for someone working, but it is a much bigger issue for someone driving. If they are leaving, take the keys or offer to call them a taxi.

- **Report them.** Report them to higher managers.

Poor answer A poor answer may include:

- **Jumping to an accusation.** If you jump in and accuse the person, they may become aggressive or defensive.

- **Telling them off only.** You cannot just tell them off and leave the situation. They are putting lives at risk by drink driving, and this needs to be addressed.

- **Dealing with it now.** It may be wise to send them home via taxi, and then deal with the situation later when they are in a sober and fit state.

MMI Station: Making Mistakes

Station Brief: You are doing a ward round in Royal Preston Hospital, Manchester. You notice that the doctor has prescribed a drug which the patient is allergic to. You also see the doctors signature on the prescription. **How should you react in this situation? Who is the governing body which regulates how doctors should act in these situations? (Part 1 of 2)**

Good answer A good answer may include:

- **Find out if the patient has taken the drug.** You need to subtly find out the patient has taken the drug. If so, the patient needs to go to A&E urgently.

- **Don't panic the patient.** You don't want to make the patient stressed without knowing whether they have actually taken the drug.

- **Speak to the doctor.** If the doctor is local, speak to him immediately. There may be a reason he has prescribed this drug.

Poor answer A poor answer may include:

- **Reporting immediately.** Reporting the situation may be useful to do later, however in the short term the patient is your first priority.

- **Alarming the patient.** You need to find a balance between withholding information and scaring the patient.

- **Ignoring it. It could be that the doctor is aware of the allergy and has checked if the drug is safe.** However, you do not know this, so you can't assume everything is okay.

You are doing a ward round in Royal Preston Hospital, Manchester. You notice that the doctor has prescribed a drug which the patient is allergic to. You also see the doctors signature on the prescription. **How would you deal with making a mistake as a doctor? (Part 2 of 2)**

Good answer A good answer may include:

- **Remain calm.** It is important to stay calm and composed, rather than panicking.

- **Maintain faith in the medical profession.** Doctors can make mistakes on a day-to-day basis. Of course, at times it is appropriate to tell the patient of mistakes, but its not necessary every small time there is an error not compromising health (e.g. you signed the wrong box in the patient notes). Otherwise patients could lose faith in the medical profession.

- **Learn!** You want to come across as someone who is eager to learn and take on board feedback.

Poor answer A poor answer may include:

- **'I wouldn't make mistakes'.** You might be a great clinician, but the interviewer doesn't want to hear this! You don't want to be arrogant. Instead, explain what you would do if mistakes occurred.

- **Become stressed.** Some people are too open, and might say that they hate making mistakes and get emotional when they do.

MMI Station: Ethics in the News

Station Brief: Is there an ethical case in the news recently which has interested you? What issues did it raise? Why do you think it stuck out to you?

Good answer A good answer may include:

- **Explain it clearly** - don't just jump in and start giving your opinion. Explain the article properly, set the scene, and then move into a discussion.

- **Reflecting** - giving an actual reflection beyond just paraphrasing the article.

- **Opinionated** - giving an opinion, perhaps even disagreeing with the article at hand.

Poor answer A poor answer may include:

- **Non-ethical article** - the question clearly asks for an ethical article.

- **Paraphrasing** - just explaining not discussing

- **Controversial** - trying too hard to give an opinion and being controversial instead

- **Not answering all elements of the question** - they have asked 3 sub questions, so make sure to address each of them within your time!

Examiner's Tip - Your article doesn't have to be medical, but its good if it is. When you discuss your article, it could be useful to spend 1-2m explaining the article, then the remaining time discussing what issues it raised and why it stuck out. Try to give an opinion, but don't give controversial opinions by accident!

MMI Station: Confidentiality and Patient Management

Station Brief: You are a GP, and your patient comes in to see you. The appointment is just a general check-up, but during your conversation he reveals that he is regularly taking illicit drugs. **What would you do? Should you report him?**

Good answer A good answer may include:

- **Find out the extent.** How strong are the drugs - e.g. marijuana is very different to heroin. How often is he taking them? This will determine the threat posed by the drugs. Try to find out how the drugs are affecting his health.

- **Encourage him to stop and educate him.** You should explain clearly the health negatives of these drugs. You should also give safety tips if he refuses to stop - e.g. tell him not to re-use needles, as this can lead to infection.

- **Offer support.** Don't be too hard on him, he needs support. He trusts you, so you should not judge. Ask him why he is taking the drugs and get to the root of the problem. You can also advise him of community programmes where he can get support if he is addicted.

- **You don't HAVE to report him.** As a doctor, you do not legally need to report illegal activity unless the patient or someone else is in imminent danger. The GMC states that you are allowed to report illegal activity to the police, but you do not have a legal obligation to. If you do wish to report, you should try to get the patient consent, and should only overwrite this if there is a threat to the public. If the man has a child, and you believe that the child is under threat, you may need to report the man if he does not consent to stop.

MMI Station: Misdiagnosis and Difficult Situations

Station Brief: As a results of misdiagnosis a patient has died.

What would you do in this scenario? (Part 1 of 3)

Good answer A good answer may include:

- **Investigate what happened.** A full review needs to be done to understand why there was a misdiagnosis.

- **Apologise to the family.** Apologise profusely to the family and offer support.

- **Learn and reflect.** Use this opportunity as a learning curve to improve for the future.

- **Take a break.** If you need to, take a short break from medicine to re-coup.

- **Inform seniors.** You need to inform seniors of this mistake so that a review is done.

Poor answer A poor answer may include:

- **Hide the mistake.** You cannot lie and hide the mistake.

- **Blame someone else.** This is unethical and poor behaviour.

- **Leave medicine.** You will go through difficult times, you can't quit this easily!

- **Blame yourself too much.** You may have made an error, but it may have been a tricky diagnosis. The patient may not have survived even with the correct diagnosis.

As a results of misdiagnosis a patient has died.

Apart from misdiagnosis, why might you experience stress in medicine? (Part 2 of 3)

Good answer A good answer may include:

- **Dealing with bad news -** giving bad news to patients can be quite difficult

- **Setbacks -** e.g. if a patient dies, it can be difficult to cope with

- **Time pressures -** relate to your work experience, e.g. in GP you may have seen how stressful it is to manage a different patient every 10 minutes whilst still providing a high quality of care

- **Constant learning -** although exciting, it can be stressful to continuously have to learn and evolve

- **Hospital setting -** seeing so many people and standing around all day can be quite stressful

- **Lack of resources -** there may not be enough staff members, hospital beds or funding in the NHS

- **Difficult patients -** some patients may be rude, some may sue you.

- **Long hours -** hours can be quite difficult, especially in FY1 and FY2 where you may have night shifts.

As a results of misdiagnosis a patient has died.

Do you think your time at St. George's Medical School will help you cope with situations with this? Why? (Part 3 of 3)

Good answer A good answer may include:

- **Clinical exposure.** In later years, being in hospital, I can learn how to manage patients.

- **Experience.** I am likely to see a similar situation of a doctor making a grave mistake during medical school. I can learn from it and see how he / she deals with the error.

- **Communication skills.** I will improve my communication skills through group teaching, hospital clinics and university societies. So I can better deal with speaking with the family.

- **Hard work and drive.** The work ethic and passion for medicine needed for the course will drive me as a person, and will enable me to withstand tough times like a patient dying.

MMI Station: Social Media

Station Brief: The use of social media websites such as Facebook is now widespread amongst the public, students and healthcare professionals. Is it appropriate for medical students and doctors to use such websites? **(Part   1   of   3)**

Good answer A good answer may include:

- **Yes it is.** Don't say that doctors and medical students cannot use social media! It is a good way to socialise with people and have a life outside of medicine.

- **Be careful of posting wrong things.** If a doctor posted something offensive, then his / her patients may lose trust. It can also reflect badly on the NHS.

- **Don't post about patients.** If a doctor posted about a patient, it is a breach of confidentiality. So they need to be careful with this.

- **Don't be-friend patients.** It isn't very appropriate for doctors to be-friend patients, even if they add the doctor on Facebook and insist on being friends. It is important to maintain a professional relationship.

Poor answer A poor answer may include:

- **Dismissing social media.** Don't dismiss social media completely - many doctors and medical students use it, so you can tell it is allowed.

- **Failure to discuss patient interaction.** This question is less interested about doctors interacting amongst themselves, and more about doctor and patient interaction on social media.

How would you advise a doctor who is wondering whether to accept one of their patients as a friend on a social media website such a Facebook? Why? **(Part 2 of 3)**

Good answer A good answer may include:

- **He should not.** It is unprofessional of the doctor to accept the patient on Facebook, so he should not.

- **Explain to the patient.** It may be worth explaining the reasons to the patient at the next appointment. This will mean that the patient doesn't feel embarrassed or insecure.

Should medical students and doctors always declare their profession/professional status when interacting with others on a social media website? Why? **(Part 3 of 3)**

Good answer A good answer may include:

- **They don't have to.** Declaring your profession is a personal preference. Some people don't want to display this, so they should not be forced to.

- **They should not use their profession for leverage.** At the same time, it is worth discussing that doctors should not use their profession as leverage on social media - e.g. to impress members of the opposite sex, or for blackmail.

MMI Station: Patient Refusing Treatment

Station Brief: Dorothy, an 83 year old lady is suffering from community acquired pneumonia. She has been admitted into hospital and is refusing all treatment. She claims "I just want to die, let me die peacefully". One of her son's James appreciates his mother's position and is not willing to change it however Dorothy's daughter Alexandra wants her mother to keep fighting and wants her to continue having her medication. **What are some of the key issues raised here? What do you know about consent? (Part 1 of 2)**

Good answer A good answer may include:

- **Is Dorothy competent?** If Dorothy is competent and in a fit state, she has the ultimate decision. If she is not competent, you have to refer the decision on to her next to kin, which would be on her medical records.

- **The patient has the final decision.** If Dorothy is competent, then you cannot force her to have the treatment, even if you think it is in her best interests.

- **You can convince her.** You are allowed to explain why its a good idea to have treatment, although you cannot force her.

Poor answer A poor answer may include:

- **Forcing her to have treatment. It is** wrong to force Dorothy to take treatment if she is competent and does not want the treatment.

- **Ignoring her children.** You cannot just dismiss her children. You can speak to Dorothy, explain the views of James and Alexandra. If Dorothy is not competent, then the views of her two children become very important.

- **Poor knowledge of ethics.** Some students have not done their revision and have a poor understanding of medical ethics.

You are a junior doctor and your consultant sees Dorothy. Your consultant tells you to give Dorothy the medication as he says "she doesn't know what she is talking about". **How should you as a junior doctor respond in this scenario? (Part 2 of 2)**

Good answer A good answer may include:

- **Find out more information.** It is important to find out what the doctor means by this. It could be interpreted as meaning that Dorothy is non-competent, and the medical team are making a decision in her best interests (beneficence). Alternatively, it could just be that the doctor is ignoring Dorothy's requests and is overriding her, which would be illegal.

- **Don't be scared to reprimand the constant.** If the consultant is overriding Dorothy's autonomy, then you shouldn't be scared to tell him, and potentially report this incident to someone senior.

Poor answer A poor answer may include:

- **Being scared of the consultant.** Even though the consultant is more senior than you, it is also your responsibility to respect the patient's rights of autonomy.

- **Poor knowledge of ethics.** Some students may not see anything wrong with this order, and would just reply with 'I would give her the medication'. The best way to improve with ethical scenarios is to practice, practice and practice!

MMI Station: Confidentiality

Station Brief: Rishi is a 53 year old man who has been suffering from pain on his sexual organs and suspects he has herpes simplex virus. His wife, Reshma is concerned and wants him to visit the doctor (you). Rishi and Reshma both enter the consultation room and Rishi asks to speak to you privately. He discloses that he has been having an affair, and suspects that he has transmitted herpes to his wife. Reshma storms into the room asking what Rishi has told you, claiming she has a right to know. **How do you approach this situation? What is the importance of confidentiality? When can confidentiality be breached? (Part 1 of 2)**

Good answer A good answer may include:

- **Respect Rishi's confidentiality.** You cannot just tell the wife what Rishi has told you. You have to respect his confidentiality first of all.

- **First ask Rishi to tell his wife.** You have to try to convince Rishi to tell his wife about the STI. You have to give him the opportunity to tell her.

- **If he refuses, tell the wife.** If he refuses, THEN you can override him and tell the wife, because Rishi is endangering her by withholding information.

- **The affair may not be relevant.** It is hard to tell if the affair is relevant to this situation. If it is, then the wife has to be told. If it isn't, you may just have to disclose the herpes.

- **Act calmly and support both parties.** This is obviously a very emotional situation. Your first job should be to calm down both parties. It may be best to speak to Rishi and Reshma separately in two different consultations.

Reshma tells you that she has been suffering from depression, and a triggering factor was that she once caught   Rishi   texting   another   woman.

Does this change the situation? (Part 2 of 2)

Good answer A good answer may include:

- **It doesn't change the confidentiality issue.** Your responsibility is to ensure that there is no external threat to another person. Rishi has herpes, and if he refuses to tell his wife, his wife is in danger. Therefore you must break confidentiality, regardless of whether the wife is depressed.

- **You can provide social support to the wife.** You should speak to the wife about her issues. Be supportive, kind and understanding. You can also refer the wife on to specialist support team.

NHS Hot Topics

Station Brief: There has been a significant drop in nurses coming from the EU working in the NHS. So much so that the royal college of nursing have said that Brexit puts an "immediate risk to the provision of safe and effective care". How might the shortage of nursing staff affect healthcare in the NHS?

Good answer A good answer may include:

- **Increasing Demands.** Nurses are especially important now because of our ageing population (long term illness and repeated hospital admissions)

- **Overworking of Staff.** Leads to burnout among present nurses due to understaffing issue so less likely to recruit more nurses in the future

- **Role of Nurses.** Could argue that nurses play bigger role in patient care as they actually are the backbone of NHS, so with fewer numbers care is compromised

Poor answer A poor answer may include:

- **Ignoring their role.** Nurses truly are extremely important and the current lack of nurses is affecting patient safety.

- **Not coming up with a solution.** e.g. reinstating the NHS bursary to fund more nurses training, fast track courses

- **Lack of terminology.** You want to really show you're keeping up to date with what is in the news around the nursing crisis.

Station Brief: The Charlie Gard case was a case that divided the public's opinion and received extensive media coverage. Discuss what influence cases like this might have on the NHS as well as the medical profession.

Good answer A good answer may include:

- **Media coverage** – the facts presented in the media may lack factual accuracy, misleading the general public. The way the information is presented may also influence the people's perception of the case and their opinion on it.

- **Transparency** – as medical professionals we have to be transparent about our decisions. During cases like this, other doctors working in similar environments might find themselves under increased public scrutiny and stress even though they are not directly involved in the case.

- **Trust in the medical profession** – cases like this often result in decrease of trust in healthcare professionals and increased negative attitudes towards the staff.
- **Debate** – the complexity of the Carlie Gard case led to extensive discussions. ****Making doctors reconsider the principles by which decisions are made and the best course of action.

Poor answer A poor answer may include:

- **Complexity of the case** – not acknowledging that the Charlie Gard's case was complicated dividing not only the public but also the healthcare professionals.
- **Best interests** – forgetting that the medical professionals are acting in the best interest of the child.
- **Being judgmental** – assuming that either the medical professionals or Charlie Gard's parents are automatically in the wrong.
- **Prominent figures** – even though, famous people such as the Pope have stated their opinion on the case, we cannot follow their views blindly and need to consider the expertise of the healthcare professionals.
- **Not acknowledging the effect of the case on attitudes towards health staff** – cases like this often result in increased negative attitudes towards staff, making them feel uncomfortable, stressed and endangered at work.

Additional Discussion Points

- What causes patient-doctor relationships to breakdown to the degree that legal action is required?
- How would you approach this situation?
- How would you prevent escalating to court involvement?
- Would the ethics of these cases be different if it were an adult involved?

Marking Criteria	Candidate makes no reference to this (0)	Candidate makes some reference to (1)	Candidate formulates an eloquent answer and provides good reasoning behind answer (2)
Candidate introduces themselves.			
Candidate gives a clear outline of what the case entailed.			
Candidate states that the case was complicated.			
Candidate explores different views on this case and discusses why they thought a specific course of action should have been undertaken.			
Candidate acknowledges that cases like this have influence on both the NHS and the medical professionals.			
Candidate says that media play an important role in such cases.			
Candidate discusses the impact it might have on the confidence level in healthcare professionals.			
Candidate mention and/or refers to acting in the best interests of the patient.			
Candidate discusses the impact such cases have on the working conditions of doctors.			
Candidate states a conclusion.			

Station Brief: Consider this cartoon used in a newspaper discussion about the 7 Day NHS proposals. Under the scheme, local GP surgeries are to be open on Saturdays and Sundays. The Royal College of GPs believe that it is unachievable, and will destabilise other services. You are pitching to Jeremy Hunt, to explain why it is a bad idea. The interviewer will play Jeremy Hunt, and argue for the 7 Day NHS.

Interviewer Instructions

You are pretending to be Jeremy Hunt. Argue for 7 day NHS:

- Will improve patient services on weekends, which can sometimes be poor

- Consultants currently can opt out of non-emergency work at weekends. But this can be detrimental to the NHS.

- Doctors wages can be increased to compensate, and this may encourage some doctors

Good answer A good answer may include:

- **More stress.** It will lead to more stress for doctors, leading to poorer morale and worse efficiency

- **More mistakes.** Tired doctors will make more mistakes

- **Less desire to be a doctor.** There is already a growing negative stigma against some parts of the job of a doctor, so it could reduce applications

- **Discussion of wages.** The NHS hasn't got funds to pay higher wages on weekends

Poor answer A poor answer may include:

- **Agree too much.** Argue the pro points by accident, or agree to much with Mr. Hunt.

- **Simplistic arguments**. Lack of structure or overly simplistic arguments - e.g. 'it'll make doctors tired' without implications on patient care or doctor morale

- **Lack of knowledge**. Assuming that currently there is no medical care on weekends - e.g. A&E is still open!

Golden Tip: Don't be scared to think outside the box and try to actually provide a solution. For example, you could argue against a 7 day NHS, but state that if it does happen, there should be much higher wages for doctors to compensate.

MMI Station: Doctors Striking

Station Brief: Read this article, and then discuss whether you believe doctors should be allowed to strike?

The British Medical Association has been accused of "playing politics", by the prime minister, after the union announced a week of strikes in England. Theresa May said the contract being imposed on junior doctors was "safe" and urged them to put patients first. It comes as hospitals are drawing up contingency plans for the five consecutive days of all-out stoppages, which get under way on 12 September.

The BMA said it had no choice as its members were opposed to the contract. She called on the union to call off the strikes, adding that the NHS had "record levels of funding" and "more doctors than we've seen in its history". She went on: "The government is putting patients first, the BMA should be putting patients first - not playing politics."

Pros of Striking

- **Right to strike** - doctors have a right to strike like other professions. All employees should have the right to carry out industrial action against their employer

- **Striking works** - striking is an effective way to be heard and noticed

- **Non-emergency care can be rearranged** - If non-emergency departments strike, then impact is not as high

- **Maintains morale of NHS staff** - Stopping striking would lead to poor morale amongst NHS staff

- **Long term vs short term impact** - cancelled operations and reduced access to services will affect patients. But, any new contract must protect junior doctors, as well as patients.

Cons of Striking

- **Duty to patients** - doctors have a duty to patients, and some patients will suffer from lack of treatment

- **Creates backlog** - the NHS waiting times are already high without backlog from missed days

- **Hippocratic Oath** - doctors have an obligation to the Hippocratic oath to save lives above all else

- **Public perception -** striking can lead to poor public perception of doctors. Patients may lose in trust in doctors as they may feel that doctors striking represents a lack of dignity and care for patients

- **Harmful if emergency staff strike** - Striking of emergency doctors is harmful

MMI Station: Junior Doctor Contract

Station Brief: After years of negotiation between the Department of Health and the British Medical Association, the junior doctors accepted a new contract in June 2019. Explain how the new contract meets the needs of the junior doctors and allows them to improve patient care.

Good answer A good answer may include:

- **Limits long repeat shifts** - Identifies limits on the number of long shifts, of up to 13 hours, they can work in a row

- **Doctors less overworked** - Explains how this limit will prevent doctors becoming overworked and therefore will allow doctors to treat patients to best of their ability

- **No more "pay-to-stay"** - Identifies improvements in rest and safety entitlements, with no more pay-to-stay when too tired to drive and explain how it improves doctor quality of life

- **Pay rise to incentivise doctors** - Identifies a pay-rise averaging 2% for each of the next four years, beginning in 2020 and explains that increase payment incentivises doctors to stay in NHS

Poor answer A poor answer may include:

- **Little knowledge** - offers little knowledge on new junior doctor contract

- **Superficial with little analysis** - doesn't analyse the effects of the new contract on patient care and doctor quality of life

- **Makes assumptions -** e.g. doctors would work badly if the contract went ahead.

MMI Station: Sugar Tax

Station Brief: Please analyse the data given here on the impact of sugar tax, and answer the following questions:

Q1/3 What do you see on the data here?

Good answer A good answer may include:

- **Use actual figures** from the image.

- **Being succinct** to ensure you cover all three points within the 5 minutes.

- **Picking out information** that you think is relevant and explaining why you think it is relevant.

- **Referencing the image** when you are asked questions.

Poor answer A poor answer may include:

- **Reading off what you see**, instead of explaining it in detail.

- **Being distracted** by the large amount of information.

- **Not using exact values**

- **Not going beyond** the information provided and just stating facts

Q2/3 What do you know about the sugar tax?

Good answer A good answer may include:

- **Acknowledge two sides** to the issue

- **Structured answer**. Goes through the two sides in a structured order, always relating back to the question

- **Gives a conclusion.** Concludes on an opinion based on considering these arguments and their interaction

- **References international taxes.** Reference to Mexico, France, Hungary or Chile as a case study / example

Poor answer A poor answer may include:

- **Unbalanced argument.** Giving just one side of the argument when asked about your opinion on sugar tax.

- If you haven't read up on sugar tax, don't show them!

Q3/3 What are your opinions on it?

PROS of Sugar Tax

- **International case studies.** A similar sugar tax was enforced in Mexico to an initial decrease in soft drink purchases and intake.

- **Increased funding.** Increased revenue increases spending power in areas that require funding e.g. NHS, or decrease price of healthier items

- **Less spent on treatments.** It also decreases expenditure on treatments for conditions a high sugar diet would cause e.g. Type 2 Diabetes

- **Ethical arguments:** governments have a moral obligation to ensure the health of their citizens (beneficence / non-maleficence)

- **High sugar intake is linked to higher levels of obesity**, diabetes and tooth decay therefore the sugar tax may help reduce this

Poor answer A poor answer may include:

- **Soft drink purchases and intake have since rebounded;** we could increase the tax, but would this just repeat the cycle?

- **Socioeconomic inequality.** A tax hits those with lower socioeconomic status much harder than those who are more affluent – is this fair?

- **Better to encourage healthy eating.** Would a programme encouraging healthy eating be more popular than a programme which discourages unhealthy eating?

- **Ethical arguments:** governments should not be paternalistic, like how doctors should not be. Citizens, like patients, have a right to choose (autonomy). Should we instead educate people on in the impacts of a sugar rich diet and leave them to choose?

- **Not the only cause of obesity.** Obesity is simply being attributed to high sugar intake and calories through diet alone rather than holistically through lifestyle modifications such as exercising and overall diet.

MMI Station: Dr Bawa Garba

Station Brief: Discuss Dr Bawa Garba's case. Do you think doctors' license to practice should be taken away when they make a medical mistake?

Good answer A good answer may include:

- **Complexity of the situation** – Dr Bawa Garba's case was complicated with presence of both human medical errors as well as IT system failures. A good answer shows an understanding of it.

- **Reasons when medical license might be taken away** – sometimes the medical license is taken away from doctors and there are valid reasons for that like unethical behaviour, medical malpractice, substance abuse and sexual misconduct.

- **General public's trust in the medical profession** – the case had an impact on how the public views healthcare staff, in particular it reduced their level of confidence in medical professionals.

- **Medical malpractice** – it happens when the medical professional causes serious and avoidable harm to a patient due to negligence, omission to take action, provision of substandard quality of care. A good answer should discuss this in relation to the case.

- **Current problems experienced within the NHS** – Due to understaffing, Dr Bawa Garba was covering several wards and was responsible for too many patients. This is not an uncommon situation in the NHS and often leads to increased workload, higher stress levels experienced by the health staff as well as reduction in the quality of delivered care

Poor answer A poor answer may include:

- **Superficial answer** – not going into details or discussing just one side of the problem shows that the interviewee doesn't have a good understanding of the case.

- **Makes stuff up** – it's obvious to the examiners!

- **Fails to acknowledge what a medical mistake means** – most doctors make a mistake at one point in their medical careers; however, each mistake is different ranging from that not impacting the quality of delivered care to a medical error causing serious harm to a patient!

- **Jumps straight to conclusions** – the candidate should discuss different dimensions of both the case and the question first.

Golden Tip: in interviews, they are very unlikely to expect you to know about the specific case beforehand. For example, they would not start a question with "What do you know about Dr Bawa Garba?". Instead, they are more likely to give you a bit of background or an article excerpt, and then the good candidates should use their external knowledge to really debate the topic well.

MMI Station: Mental Health

Station Brief: Please discuss the current challenges facing mental health services provision in the UK. How would you tackle the problem of rising ill mental health in the country?

Good answer A good answer may include:

- **Investment into mental health services** – despite the government's promises, there have been substantial cuts in funding. Increasing investment could help improve the quality and availability of services.
- **Services for young people and new mother**s – these groups are particularly at risk of mental health issues. Campaigning for better health, increasing awareness of symptoms and ways to get help could all prove beneficial.
- **Workforce numbers** – NHS is currently facing a healthcare staff shortage and this is also seen across mental health services. Increasing staff numbers would greatly aid in enhancing the availability of services.
- **Education of doctors and nurses** – training health practitioners, in particular GPs, in recognising symptoms of mental health issues could aid in early identification of these symptoms and starting treatment where necessary.
- **Emergency support** – recent data has shown that emergency mental health support is lacking. Increasing numbers of all-age liaison psychiatrists in A&Es, availability of sanctuaries and crisis cafes as well as improving competency of ambulance staff in providing mental health support could all be helpful.

Poor answer A poor answer may include:

- **Assumption that mental health problems are not real** – belittling patients because of their mental health issues as well as considering their symptoms as 'made-up' in their own heads is inappropriate.
- **Discrimination** – all patients with mental health problems should be able to access the support services.
- **Making patients pay for services** – NHS is provided free of charge and patients shouldn't be charged extra for being seen earlier or out of hours.
- **Blaming the problem on e.g. politics rather than focusing on how to tackle the issue** –

while there are a lot of factors that contribute to the existing problem of mental health crisis, the question asks the candidate to discuss the current challenges and how we can address them rather than to point to who is to blame!

Marking Criteria	Candidate makes no reference to this (0)	Candidate makes some reference to (1)	Candidate formulates an eloquent answer and provides good reasoning behind answer (2)
Candidate introduces themselves appropriately.			
Candidate clearly outlines what is meant by the current mental health crisis in the UK.			
Candidate discusses different challenges faced by the mental health services and how they impact the delivery of care.			
Candidate mentions and/or refers to rising staff shortage across mental health services.			
Candidate explores the problem of inadequate investment into the services which translates onto how they are delivered.			
Candidate realises the importance of training of doctors in recognising early symptoms of mental disease			
Candidate suggests ways to tackle the mental health issues and provides examples of how they could be implemented			
Candidate states a conclusion			

MMI Station: Ageing Population

Station Brief: The UK has an ageing population (ONS, 2018k). There are nearly 12 million (11,989,322) people aged 65 and above in the UK of which: o 5.4 million people are aged 75. How do you think we can meet the challenges of an ageing population?

Good answer A good answer may include:

- **Issues of an ageing population** - fragile (falls, injuries), disability, co-morbidities, admission to hospital, need for long-term care, alzheimers / dementia, loneliness

- **Improved health and social care services** – more district nurses, a robust systematic method for evaluating and addressing individual, holistic needs - to design a personalised care planning

- **Charities e.g. Age UK** – raise awareness, educate / empower elderly citizens

- **Reduce the amount of time spent in hospitals** – housing, support networks (family, friends, neighbours). Also working closely with GPs, psychiatrists, district nurses and other healthcare professionals to design a MDT for elderly patients

- **Present opportunities for elderly** - volunteering, community activities, buddy-schemes, social clubs, help people stay in work

- **Good quality housing** - ensuring there's safe and warm housing, a significant number of admissions are from excess cold hazards and falls – home aids / adaptations e.g. handrails, ramps, level-access showers

- **Public health campaigns** – elderly in particular may have had long-term habits e.g. smoking, drinking alcohol, drugs, unhealthy diet hence it is more challenging and difficult to alter their behaviours, more campaign specific to help such challenges

MMI Station: Free Healthcare

Station Brief: The NHS has famously been 'free at the point of delivery'. What are the pros and cons of having a free healthcare system, such as the NHS, compared to one that charges?

Pros of Free Healthcare

- **Healthcare for everyone.** Those with less income can still afford healthcare. Access to healthcare should, some argue, be a human right.

- **Reduces disease burden.** For example, being diagnosed with cancer is hard enough, but having to pay £100,000 in medical fees can worsen the problem.

- **Improves public health.** If everyone receives good healthcare, the country is healthier, people are happier and the workforce is more efficient (e.g. less sick days).

Cons of Free Healthcare

- **Less competition.** With less private influence, there are less companies competing and hence less drive to improve healthcare. The NHS can become complacent.

- **Financial limitation.** The NHS is always short on money and resources, which can lead to poor quality of care.

- **High tax burden.** A large amount of tax is paid to the NHS. Some capitalists argue that it is unfair on those who can afford healthcare and have to pay for others.

MMI Station: Antibiotic Resistance

Station Brief: Antibiotic resistance is on the rise both in the UK and globally. Discuss why this is the case and the implications this might have in the treatment of infections in the future.

Good   answer   A   good   answer   may   include:

- **Define antibiotic resistance.** Antibiotic resistance occurs when bacteria become resistant to antibiotics, meaning that bacteria will not be killed by antibiotics.

- **Discuss increased/unnecessary prescriptions**. Antibiotics are being severely over- prescribed, leading to antibiotic resistance.

- **Explains key reasons for antibiotic resistance** e.g. inappropriate prescribing, unfinished antibiotic courses and overuse.

- **Explore future treatment of infections.** With continued antibiotic resistance, antibiotics will become ineffective at treating bacterial infections, leaving future patients with bacterial infections without an effective treatment strategy.

- **Consider multiple viewpoints.** A thoughtful candidate might realise that doctors and pharmacists are prescribing increasingly high amounts of antibiotics, whilst patients are frequently requesting antibiotics for suspected infections. Both are significant factors in driving antibiotic resistance.

- **Suggests some ideas for how these issues might be tackled** e.g. stricter regulations, development of new antibiotics, using a combination of antibiotics etc (or any other interesting idea).

Poor answer A poor answer may include:

- **Indicate poor understanding of the topic.** This may include not being able to understand how antibiotic resistance comes about, or not being able to suggest reasons as to why antibiotic resistance is on the rise.

- **Show little explanation of future implications.** If the candidate does not mention future implications of antibiotic resistance, they are missing a key point of the brief, which asks the candidates to use their knowledge of the topic to think critically.

- **Place blame.** A poor candidate may place blame fully on one group of people (ex. doctors, for over-prescribing) without exploring viewpoints as to why this might be the case. Placing blame on one singular group without understanding their rationale may come across as judgmental.

- **Unaware of the current antibiotic issues** and is unsure of the scientific basis behind the development of antibiotic resistance.

- **Explains concepts in layman's terms** e.g. "Using antibiotics makes stronger bacteria grow".

- **No clear suggestions.** Cannot produce any realistic or creative ideas about how this resistance might be tackled e.g. just saying that we should prescribe antibiotics isn't providing a clear answer as to HOW this should be done.

MMI   Station: Vaccinations

Station Brief: In your opinion, should childhood vaccinations be made compulsory? Outline why you have made this decision, as well as the reasons why some people may disagree with you. Describe and explain any additional changes that you would make regarding childhood vaccinations in the UK.

YES, they should be made compulsory:

- **Protects children** – children whose parents decide against vaccination are at risk of infection.

- **Protects vulnerable groups** – those who have reduced immunity, such as those on immunosuppressants, rely on herd immunity. When parents choose not to vaccinate their children it leaves these people at risk.

NO, they should <u>NOT</u> be made compulsory:

- **Contradicts patient autonomy** – this would cause a lot of backlash as many parents would feel that they should be responsible for decisions involving their child and no one else.

- **Loss of trust in NHS** – patients may be concerned about other treatments also being pushed on them when they go to the doctor

Raise awareness – invest money in campaigns and education in schools that spread awareness of the benefits of vaccination and diminish false claims (such as the MMR vaccine causing autism).

Poor answer A poor answer may include:

- **Unbalanced** - answer does not fully account for both sides of the argument.

- **Limited explanation/ detail** – eg. Only raising one point for either side of the argument.

- **Dismissive.** Being dismissive when describing the views of those who may disagree with their own opinion.

MMI Station: Best Interests Decisions

Station Brief: Five-year-old Tafida Raqeeb has been on life support at the Royal London Hospital since suffering a traumatic brain injury in February. Her parents have organised funding to take her to the Gaslini children's hospital in Genoa, Italy. But UK specialists had argued any further treatment would be futile. Bosses at Barts Health NHS Trust, which runs the hospital in Whitechapel, had asked the judge to rule that ending   Tafida's   life-support   was   in   her   best   interests.

1. Do you agree with the doctors or the parents and why?

2. What issues could arise by involving the court?

Agreeing with Doctors

- **Best interests.** They are acting in the best interest of the patient by not wanting to allow her condition to worsen whilst waiting for ethical approval of a new treatment.

- **Reducing her pain.** They are minimising pain for the child as it is unclear if she would be pain free.

- **Rational outlook.** Because they are less emotionally invested in the situation than the parents and so the doctors will see the situation more rationally of what is best for the patient.

- **Ethical.** They are following the pillars of medical ethics, beneficence and non-maleficence.

Agreeing with Parents

- **Potential for recovery.** Although their daughter's condition may worsen before the treatment if give, there is potential that the treatment will work and allow the girl to live a more normal life.

- **How can you judge if a life is worth living?** Their daughter will be loved regardless of whether she is on life support or not; her life will be worth living regardless.

- **Autonomy.** In terms of autonomy, the parents believe it is their decision what should happen to their baby.

Issues that Could Arise

- **Pressure on the doctors.** It could put a pressure on doctors to act in favour of the parents, even if they don't think this will be the best outcome for the patient.

- **Media impact.** Media reporting and the use of social media can create divisive opinions and harm the reputation of medical teams and the medical profession as a whole.

- **Prolongs decision making.** The legal process takes time and this delays any decision making. This lengthens the amount of time Tafida is left on life support which may not be in her best interest.

- **Ethics.** This will cause issues in terms of beneficence and non-maleficence.

MMI Station: Legalising Cannabis

Station Brief: Recently there has been significant discussion in the news regarding the use of medical cannabis to treat complex illnesses such as types of epilepsy and chronic pain. Please discuss your point of view on the subject of using medicinal cannabis.

Mark Scheme

- **Pillars of medical ethics.** A good answer will refer to the 4 pillars of medical ethics (beneficence, non-maleficence, autonomy and justice) during the course of their answer.

- **Recent developments.** An excellent candidate will be aware of the recent approval of medicinal cannabis to treat 2 types of epilepsy (Lennox Gastaut syndrome and Dravet syndrome) as well as spasticity occurring as a result of MS.

- **Consideration of cost**. It costs £5k-£10k to treat with medicinal cannabis per patient per year. Given that the approved drugs will only be of benefit to relatively few people, it should be considered as to whether the treatment offers value for money in comparison to traditional treatments.

- **Safety implications.** Discuss the possible safety implications of using drugs containing medicinal cannabis and whether the drugs will cause severe unintended consequences.

- **Current legality.** The legality of such medications should also be considered. By approving medication for some diseases and not others do you risk an increase in people obtaining drugs from non reputable sources?

- **One sided.** A poor answer will focus on one side of the argument without due consideration for opposing points of view. Candidates should avoid falling into the trap of criticising the use using the justification of it being 'drugs'.

- **Avoid appearing judgemental.** A poor answer will show judgement or discrimination to a subset of patients which are likely to be encountered by the candidate in their future career.

MMI Station: Resource Allocation

Station Brief: You are the Health Secretary. You want to reduce A&E waiting times. Outline how would you like to achieve it and which areas would invest in for your project to be successful.

Good answer A good answer may include:

- **Patient education** – educating patients when visiting A&E is appropriate and when it is more appropriate to visit an Urgent Care Centre or GP reduces the number of patients coming to an the   Emergency   Department   with   less   urgent   conditions.

- **IT and healthcare innovations** – introducing digital systems to help triage patients could speed up the admissions process in the A&E

- **Recruit more staff and increase retention** - emergency departments struggle to recruit and retain enough staff to fill the job vacancies. Improving work conditions, introducing incentives and maintaining staff job satisfaction could all help in achieving this.

- **Improving access to hospital beds and diagnostics** – commonly the waiting times are increased because of lack of hospital beds or reduced access to diagnostic tests. Investment in this area could facilitate faster seeing of patients by the hospital staff as well as getting a quicker diagnosis.

- **Access to GP care** – improving access to GP services could reduce the number of people who come to A&E with non-urgent conditions only because they are not able to secure a GP appointment

Poor answer A poor answer may include:

- **Making patients pay before letting them access A&E** – access to A&E should not be based to ability to pay as the emergency departments are meant to treat people with life-threatening conditions. Moreover, NHS is still a free service.

- **Discrimination** – any patient with life-threatening symptoms should be able to access A&E

- **Bad investment ideas** – not supporting under resourced A&E departments might not be an effective solution in motivating them to reduce waiting times if they are not capable of doing so purely because of financial reasons and lack of resources or funding

- **Admitting patients based on the order they got to the A&E in** – triage is more appropriate and helps identify patients with life-threatening conditions faster. This allows for seeing them earlier and improves their outcomes.

MMI Station: Whistleblowing

Station Brief: Discuss this article. Why are whistleblowers important? What impact will them being shamed have on healthcare? What impact will it have on the people concerned?

https://www.independent.co.uk/news/health/gosport-scandal-latest-inquiry-jane-barton-whistleblowers-deaths-war-memorial-hospital-a8410761.html

Hundreds of NHS whistleblowers suffered repercussions from colleagues and bosses last year, figures show – raising fears that hospital staff could be deterred from reporting problems. Campaigners warned the issue could lead to a repeat of the Gosport scandal, after it was revealed on Wednesday that 456 patients were killed by unnecessary opiate painkillers at one hospital despite nurses raising concerns as far back as 1991. Some 356 whistleblowers in 2017-18 said they had experienced repercussions, ranging from "subtle" persecution by closing off career opportunities through to being fired unjustly.

Patient safety experts and whistleblowers said that deaths like those at Gosport War Memorial Hospital were likely to be happening in other hospitals as staff still could not raise concerns freely. On Thursday healthcare safety academic Professor Brian Jarman told BBC News the reality for whistleblowers in the NHS was "they're fired, gagged and blacklisted", and a third of staff say they would be concerned about speaking out.

Good answer A good answer may include:

- **Report problems.** Whistleblowers are important as they report poor standard of care or problems in the system. If they are not raised by whistleblowers, they may never be spotted.

- **To keep doctors on alert.** If doctors do not have anyone to answer to, they may begin to slack. If they know that they may be reported if they provide poor care, they are more incentivised to work hard and provide the high quality of care they should

- **Reference cases.** It is useful to reference some previous cases. For example, Harold Shipman was a GP who committed many murders. This is an excellent example of how doctors can go astray and commit criminal acts if not controlled.

- **Reduce the number of reports.** If healthcare professionals see problems, they may be scared to report them because they will be shamed in their workplace. This will lead to people not reporting, and therefore problems will not be addressed. The quality of care may remain poor, and patients may suffer as a result.

- **Negatively impact those who do report.** Whistleblowers who still do report may find that they have to sacrifice their happiness. They may feel uneasy and unsettled at their workplace, and be bullied by managers.

MMI Station: Key Issues in Health care

Station Brief: This station is focused on some key issues in today's NHS. The average age of the UK population has continued to rise over the past 20 years. **Why is the ageing population medically important?**

Good   answer   A   good   answer   may   include:

- **Shows success of healthcare -** the ageing population shows that people are living longer, which is a positive sign of the progress in the UK healthcare system.

- **Increased stress on NHS resources.** Elderly people tend to need more healthcare, so an ageing population adds strain to the NHS funds and resources.

- **Increased incidence of certain diseases.** Some conditions, such as Type 2 Diabetes, increase in likelihood as one gets older. With the ageing population, conditions such as Type 2 Diabetes have become more prevalent in the NHS.

- **Increased retirement age.** One benefit of the ageing population is that people are retiring later because they have longer to live. This means that experienced consultants retire later, which helps increase the supply of high-quality doctors in the NHS.

MMI Station: NHS Budget

Station Brief: 'Don't blame the NHS for denying vital medication. Blame the pharma companies hooked on huge profits'

Is it ethical for drug companies to charge the NHS for treatments? **(Part 1 of 3)**

YES IT IS ETHICAL

- **Yes, profit drives research.** If drug companies had little profit, they have less incentive to conduct research.

- **Yes, profit drives competition.** The more profitable the market, the more drug companies there are, and this competition forces each company to be the best they can be.

- **Yes, to cover costs.** At the very least drug companies need to cover their costs. The amount of profit they should make can be debated, however.

NO IT IS UNETHICAL

- **No, it strains NHS resources.** The NHS has limited money as it is, so drug costs will add to this.

- **No, it can lead to a shortage of drugs.** Some patients may not be able to get enough drugs because they aren't available in large enough quantity in the NHS.

- **No, they make too much profit.** Its fine for them to make some profit, but currently they are making luxurious profit margins which is unfair on the NHS and the taxpayer.

'Don't blame the NHS for denying vital medication. Blame the pharma companies hooked on huge   profits'

Drug companies often have patents on drugs, meaning they have a 'legal copyright' over the drug. What issues do you think this could pose? **(Part 2 of 3)**

Good answer A good answer may include:

- **Leads to high prices.** The company with the patent can develop a monopoly (total power in the market), meaning that they are free to set high prices. There's no price competition.

- **Leads to inefficiencies.** If there is only one company producing a drug, they are less incentivised to be efficient.

- **Can lead to shortages.** It can lead to shortages of drugs if that particular company is not meeting demand.

- **Less scope for research.** If there were no patents, when a new drug comes out, many companies could build on the treatment and develop improved versions. But instead, patents restrict research to just the single company with the patent.

'Don't blame the NHS for denying vital medication. Blame the pharma companies hooked on huge profits'

Should the NHS charge patients for things like IVF which are expensive? **(Part 3 of 3)**

Good answer A good answer may include:

- **Yes, it is non-essential.** These treatments are not life-saving, so they should be charged for.

- **The NHS needs to draw a line.** The NHS cannot give everything for free. By charging for IVF, they can re-allocate funds elsewhere - e.g. provide more insulin for diabetics.

Poor answer A poor answer may include:

- **No, the NHS is free at the point of delivery.** Charging for IVF would undermine the long-standing principles and values of the NHS.

- **No, IVF is not 'non-essential'.** The right to have a child is quite important. Things like plastic surgery should not be provided for free, but IVF should be.

- **No, instead of charging the NHS should just no provide it.** The NHS could just provide minimal IVF, and people can go to private medicine instead. This way, the NHS don't undermine their principles.

MMI Station: Charitable Donation to NHS

Station Brief: If you had £1 million to spend on healthcare related charities, where would you donate this? Why would you donate here? What is the biggest challenge facing the NHS?

Good answer A good answer may include:

- Focusing on where there is a lack of funding e.g. mental health (only recently increased due to the new 2018 budget), Alzheimer's (Receives 3% of the investment cancer receives)

- Mentioning the ageing population as a big challenge, people are living longer with increased co-morbidities such as diabetes and obesity.

Poor answer A poor answer may include:

- Donating entire £1million into just one charity as it is close to you (This is reasonable, but they want to show that you know about the challenges in the NHS)

- Mentioning an important challenge but not justifying your reasoning. Explain why you think it is the biggest and bigger than other challenges.

Examiner's Tip - I would read through the recent government budget which explains how they will spend money on the NHS. Websites such as the King's Fund are also good places to look for to find out where there needs to be increased funding.

MMI Station: Article

Station Brief: Read this news article for 2 minutes, and then discuss the pros and cons of this new scheme.

The price of cheap, high-strength alcohol has gone up in Scotland as long-awaited legislation on minimum pricing comes into force.

The law, which sets a floor price for drinks depending on how many units of alcohol they contain, was passed in 2012 but has faced legal challenges. The Scottish government said the move would cut consumption and save lives. High-strength white cider and cheap own-brand vodka and whisky will see the biggest rise in prices.

Ministers said the idea was to target booze that attracted problem drinkers. They were concerned that a two-litre bottle of strong cider (7.5 abv), which contained more than the weekly recommended limit for alcohol (14 units), could be bought for as little as £2.50. It will now cost at least £7.50

Good answer A good answer may include:

- **Will reduce drinking.** Explain that the price rise will reduce drinking.

- **Less drinking reduces social issues.** Drinking can lead to more littering, noise pollution, violent behaviour.

- **Less drinking reduces health issues.** Drinking can increase risk of conditions such as liver failure, chronic kidney disease and cancer.

- **Socio-economic discussion.** Highest drinking areas tend to be regions of poorest socio-economic background. So a price rise could help reduce drinking in these 'problem' areas.

Poor answer A poor answer may include:

- **Increased cost.** Customers will be faced by yet another price rise for a common good.

- **Alcohol consumption may be inelastic.** Heavy drinkers are likely to buy alcohol regardless. If it is more expensive, they may underspend on food and other important necessities.

- **Alcohol in moderation is safe.** It may be unfair on those who have alcohol in moderation and drink safely and in a relatively healthy manner.

NHS Structure

MMI Station: GP Management

Station Brief: You are observing a GP reception, where you see several issues such as:

- Missed appointments

- Patients bored by waiting for so long

- Illness spreading in waiting room (e.g. coughs and colds)

- Babies crying and irritating others

- Sole receptionist getting stressed at having to sign every patient in

Think of ways to improve the reception to solve these issues.

Appointment Compliance

- **Charge for appointments** - charge people for missing appointments and make people pay for the next appointment. BUT, it defeats NHS principle of 'free at point of care'

- **An app for appointments** - an app to help scheduling of appointments easier

- **Make it easier to cancel** - if you could cancel by just pressing a button on an app, it might encourage people to actually let the GP practice / hospital know that they cannot attend. This would then free up the slot for someone else. Currently you have to call up, and patients may feel embarrassed or ashamed to cancel an appointment over the phone, so may instead just not turn up and still not cancel.

Patients Bored

- **Better entertainment -** more books, TV, educational programmes.

- **Improved furniture -** make the place seem a bit more exciting.

- **Improve appointment issue -** this will reduce waiting times.

Spread of Illness

- **More spacious waiting room -** reduce human to human spread.

- **Sanitary gel -** if it is already available, more gel could be available.

- **Separate rooms for very ill patients -** this would reduce spread of contagious conditions.

Babies   **Crying**

- **Separate room for babies -** so they can stay elsewhere and not make noise
- **Baby toys -** to distract them.

Sole Receptionist

- **More staff -** maybe internship students helping with bookings if another receptionist is not affordable.
- **Online booking system -** to reduce the manual bookings. There could be an app.
- **Check-in on machine -** some GP practices have self-check in via a machine to reduce receptionist work.

MMI Station: NHS Appointments

Station Brief: There are several ways to save money in the NHS. Discuss the 3 aims shown below by giving strategies to achieve each aim.

- Prevention over cure
- Appointment compliance
- Reducing prescription costs

For example, you might introduce a compulsory exercise scheme at schools to help 'prevention over cure'.

Prevention over Cure

- **Schemes for schools.** Increasing lessons and lectures about the importance of healthy eating. Increasing level of sports activities and making them compulsory.
- **Public awareness.** Raise public awareness of dangers of passive smoking
- **Schemes for workplaces.** Increased emphasis on company's to improve worker fitness - e.g. time allowance for gym. Companies have become very environmentally friendly over time, so we can follow suit with health.
- **Sugar tax.** To reduce the amount of sugary foods eaten.
- **Supermarket focus. Following on from the sugar tax, more subsidies for healthy food companies.**

Appointment Compliance

- **Charge for appointments -** charge people for missing appointments and make people pay for the next appointment. BUT, it defeats NHS principle of 'free at point of care'.

- **An app for appointments -** an app to help scheduling of appointments easier.

- **Make it easier to cancel -** if you could cancel by just pressing a button on an app, it might encourage people to actually let the GP practice / hospital know that they cannot attend. This would then free up the slot for someone else. Currently you have to call up, and patients may feel embarrassed or ashamed to cancel an appointment over the phone, so may instead just not turn up and still not cancel.

Reducing Prescription Costs

- **Reduce number of prescriptions given out.** Doctors should assess whether patients really need a prescription rather than handing them out aimlessly - impact of CCGs.

- **Educate patients.** Give patients a leaflet outlining the true costs of the medicine, and hence they are less likely to waste it.

- **Market the costs on packaging.** Display cost of prescription medicines on packets - words such as "funded by the UK Taxpayer".

- **Liaise with pharmaceuticals.** Liaise with pharmaceutical companies holding NHS to "ransom".

MMI Station: GMC Guidelines

Station Brief: "Establish and maintain good partnerships with your patients and colleagues"

What does this mean? Can you give any examples that you may have seen or any you can suggest? **(Part 1 of 3)**

Partnerships with Colleagues

- **Important to work together with colleagues.** You often have to work in multidisciplinary teams, so it is important to build partnerships with colleagues.

- **For example, a surgical team.** Each member of a surgical MDT has a different task - the surgeon, anaesthetist, nurses, physiotherapists etc.

- **For example, during shift changes.** When one doctor takes over from another, there needs to be a fluent passover of the patient details.

Partnerships with Patients

- **Build doctor-patient relationship.** GPs need to build strong relationships with their long-term patients.

- **Ensure trust.** Doctors need to build good relationships with patients to ensure trust. This will lead to patients being more open.

- **Working together.** Doctors cannot treat patients alone - e.g. they need the patient to take drugs, improve their lifestyle etc.

"Establish and maintain good partnerships with your patients and colleagues"

This is quote is a piece of guidance from the GMC's Tomorrow's Doctors. Who are the GMC? **(Part 2 of 3)**

Good answer A good answer may include:

- **General Medical Council (GMC).** Explain that they are the regulatory board.

- **'Fitness to Practice'.** Explain that doctors or medical students can receive fitness to practice warnings for bad behaviour.

GMC Guidelines

- **Knowledge, Skills and Performance.** This section is about providing a good standard of care, remaining up to date with knowledge and make the care of the patient your first concern!

- **Safety and Quality.** This section is about taking action when a patient's safety is at risk.

- **Communication, Partnership, Teamwork.** This section is about treating patients as individuals, maintaining confidentiality and to respect patients.

- **Maintaining Trust.** This section tells you not to discriminate with patients or abuse their trust. You should act with integrity.

"Establish and maintain good partnerships with your patients and colleagues"

What is the most important quality of a doctor? (Part 3 of 3)

Good answer A good answer may include:

- **Teamwork** is important as a doctor when you work in multidisciplinary teams, such as in surgery where you work with anaesthetists, nurses and other clinicians.

- **Leadership** is important as a doctor as you need to manage multidisciplinary teams, and show leadership to both the patient and colleagues.

- **Communication** is essential to build a doctor patient relationship.

- **Organisation**   is   key   for   managing   time   with   tasks.

- **Other** qualities include empathy, compassion, strong scientific knowledge, manual dexterity, calmness, organisation and more.

Examiner's Tip - For this question, it is essential to link the skill to your work experience. If you just say that 'teamwork is important', you won't score highly. You need to explain why it is important for doctors, and using your work experience is useful!

Communication & Roleplay

MMI Station: Verbal Reasoning Skilla

Station Brief: Please explain to the actor how to ride a bicycle without using any hand gestures. You must use your verbal reasoning skills, and remain patient when the actor is not understanding your instructions.

Good answer A good answer may include:

- Set out the aim of the task step by step. You can do this by speaking slowly and ensuring that you are as specific as possible.

- Noticing the interviewer is not following your step and correcting them

- Demonstrate that you are motivating by encouraging the actor and also be as patient as possible.

Poor answer A poor answer may include:

- Going straight into the task
- Using jargon and being vague
- Speaking really fast
- Getting frustrated as they don't follow your response e.g. sighing and getting frustrated.
- Being inpatient.

Examiner's Tip - This is a station you can practice with anyone even your family members and is a good way of honing your speaking skills. We recommend rehearsing this station several times as it is a universities' favourite!

MMI Station: Role Play: Communication Skills

Station Brief: You are a junior doctor and you are on ward 9N at Royal Free Hospital. You go to the doctor's notes and find a GP letter which tells you that your patient cannot take more than 10 units of insulin. You have given 22 units . You have already informed the patient but now need to speak to their daughter, Elizabeth.

Good   answer   A   good   answer   may   include:

- **Listen actively -** Use eye contact, verbal and non-verbal facilitation
- **Be calm -** stay composed and be open about the mistake
- **Show empathy -** be apologetic / empathetic
- **React well -** react well to patient's emotion
- **Come up with a solution -** Ensure they are happy with how you are dealing with the mistake.

Poor answer A poor answer may include:

- **Overly emotional -** becoming too emotional in front of the patient. This includes interrupting, being defensive and angry.
- **False hope -** protecting the patient by sugar coating the situation. Includes promising things
- **Use simple language -** speak in laymen terms rather than scientific language
- **Lack of empathy -** presenting a corporate feel rather than caring and empathising.

Examiner's Tip - One big weakness in candidates is jumping in and getting the worst out of the way with. You need to introduce yourself to the patient, and explain the background - e.g. 'As you know, your mother has been very ill and she has diabetes and takes insulin for it'.

MMI Station: Epilepsy Role Play

Station Brief: You are asked to speak to an young girl who is in the paediatric ward and has been there for over a month. She has epilepsy and has to be continually monitored. Please talk to her and discuss how epilepsy has affected her social life, family life, life experiences and her morale. Suggest some simple solutions to try to address her problems. These solutions do not necessarily need to be medical.

Issue & Potential Solution

- **Friends avoiding her -** Join support groups. Where you can speak to other people with epilepsy. They will understand your condition and will not treat you like your other friends.
- **Scared of falling during a seizure -** Wear a helmet. Many epilepsy patients wear a permanent helmet, incase they lose consciousness and fall during a seizure.
- **Cannot go on school trips / holidays -** Try UK internal trips. You can enjoy local trips

within the UK, and hopefully in the near future you can go abroad.

- **Always accompanied** - Try to see it as a positive. It can be frustrating, of course, but you always have someone to talk to. And everyone cares about you.

MMI Station: Communication Skills

Station Brief: At this station you will meet a patient with a long-term illness. You are asked to engage them in conversation and find out about the nature of their illness, how it is managed, what effect it has on their daily life and how they think it is likely to affect their life in the future.

You are **NOT** expected to play the role of a medical student, doctor or other healthcare professional – you should be yourself! The patient will be scoring you on your ability to interact with them.

Good answer A good answer may include:

- **Don't jump in** - ask the questions some intro questions to ease the conversation in.
- **Be calm** - stay calm and composed.
- **Show empathy** - be empathetic.
- **Use simple language** - speak in laymen terms rather than scientific language.
- **React well** - react well to patient's emotion.
- **Find out the information** - make sure to actually ask all of the things specified in the question.

Poor answer A poor answer may include:

- **Overly emotional** - becoming too emotional in front of the patient.
- **Lack of empathy** - presenting a corporate feel rather than caring and empathising.
- **Not covering the information** - not asking all of the questions specified.

Examiner's Tip - This station is linked to your ability to take a patient history. Taking a history is something a doctor does every day, and is an important part of medicine. Ask open ended questions to find out as much as possible.

MMI Station: Communication Role Play

Station Brief: You are speaking to a 34 year old man, Joseph, who is a widow as his husband Zaen passed away two years ago. He is currently dating another man, Alex and it is going well. However, he misses Zaen and wants to talk to Alex about him but is scared how he will react. Alex also wants to move to the countryside but Joseph wants to stay in London, and is unsure what to do.

He has come to you, his counsellor, for advice on what to do.

Good answer A good answer may include:

- **Be supportive.** Whatever Joseph decides, listen to him and support his actions. If he becomes emotional, stay calm and composed.

- **Advise him to be open.** The best strategy is for him to be open to his partner about his feelings. It may be difficult in the short term, but in the long term it will help the relationship.

- **Try to reach a compromise on location.** Advise him to speak to Alex about compromising with the location. Maybe they can live in the suburbs of London, which is a bit quieter but still close to the city.

Poor answer A poor answer may include:

- **Getting uncomfortable.** This scenario is quite different to your normal medical role play. The station is really testing your ability to comfort someone and provide advice. It is important for you to remain calm and provide useful advice.

- **Upsetting Joseph.** This is a matter of Joseph's personal life. Although he is discussing it with you, you have to remember to draw a line below telling him what to do. Do not upset him and be too authoritative.

MMI Station: Communication with people of Different Backgrounds

Station Brief: In life, you will encounter people from different backgrounds.

What have you learnt in your experience of speaking to diverse groups of people from different backgrounds? (Part 1 of 3)

Good answer A good answer may include:

- **You have to adapt your approach.**

  - e.g. you may need to speak slower for people from non-English backgrounds.

  - e.g. you may have to be more careful in your humour if people may be easily offended.

- **It is important to be accepting.** You need to accept all types of people as everyone is different and   has   their   own   story.

- **Link to experiences.** You can link to personal experiences of meeting different types of people - e.g. at school, whilst travelling etc.

Poor answer A poor answer may include:

- **Making stereotypes.** Be very, very careful not to border on racism or making stereotypes.

- **Remain positive.** Don't talk about disliking any particular group. You may prefer hanging out with people from the same background as you (thats not a bad thing!) but you want to come across as open and flexible in your ability to speak to different kings of people.

In life, you will encounter people from different backgrounds.

Why do you think this is important at a university like ours? (Part 2 of 3)

Good answer A good answer may include:

- **People come from different backgrounds.** A university like St.George's is very diverse and accepting of all backgrounds.

- **Everyone needs to feel welcome.** Everyone should feel welcomed, happy and accepted.

- **You will work with many people.** In university, you cannot just stick to one type of person. You'll have to work with different people - e.g. in tutorial groups.

In life, you will encounter people from different backgrounds.

And why do you think it is important as a doctor? (Part 3 of 3)

Good answer A good answer may include:

- **Patients and staff come from different backgrounds.** Many doctors / nurses are foreign, and so are many patients.

- **You have to adapt to culture.** For example, people from certain backgrounds may believe more in certain medicines, or certain treatments (e.g. alternative therapies).

- **You always need to be welcoming.** It is so crucial for doctors to remain welcoming to ensure that the patient opens up.

MMI Station: Communication – Role Play

Station Brief: Have a general talk to an actor playing a junior doctor. **Ask her about her experiences working as a junior doctor in the NHS. (Part 1 of 2)**

Good answer A good answer may include:

- **Be positive.** Of course it is useful to get a realistic picture, but you want to come across as enthusiastic and engaged.

- **Ask follow up questions.** Seem interested in what they are saying. If they talk about the enjoyment of speaking to patients, ask which type of patients they see.

- **Ask about her daily tasks.** It might be interesting to find out what she does on a day- to-day basis - how much responsibility is she given and how many patients does she see?

Poor answer A poor answer may include:

- **Asking about medical school.** The task is to find out about the role of a Junior Doctor, rather than her time at medical school. So don't ask questions on the wrong topic.

- **Being negative.** Don't be too negative - e.g. is is true that you have to work long hours, is the pay poor?

- **Simplistic questions.** Try to add depth to your questions. Rather than asking simple questions like 'what do you do', ask 'what type of patients do you see on a regular basis?'

You see a patient in the waiting area who is waiting for the doctor. The patient is very nervous. **Speak to them and try to calm them down. (Part 2 of 2)**

Good answer A good answer may include:

- **Stay calm.** Stay composed and calm when you speak to the patient.

- **Explain the importance of the blood test.** Explain that blood tests are a crucial tool in diagnosing conditions, and for looking at levels of vitamins / ions / antibodies etc. Re-assure the patient that its for their own good.

- **Re-assure the patient on the safety of needles.** Explain that the procedures are very safe, they have been trial and tested.

Poor answer A poor answer may include:

- **Being too forceful.** e.g. if the patient tries to leave, you can't tell them to sit down. You can try to convince them to stay, but cannot be too forceful.

- **Becoming frustrated.** It is easy to become frustrated with the patient, as to you a blood test may be a simple procedure which is harmless.

- **Poor explanation of a blood test.** Not knowing what a blood test involves, the importance of it, and not relaying this to the patient.

MMI Station: Picture Scenario

Station Brief: This man is on renal dialysis. He needs to go to the renal centre 3 times a week for 4 hours each time.

How do you think he is feeling? How would his health impact his life? (Part 1 of 2)

Good answer A good answer may include:

- **Frustrated.** He may be tired and frustrated at the continual appointments.

- **Tired.** Renal dialysis can be tiring - you have to spend 3-4 hours each time, just sitting there.

- **Demoralised.** Renal impairments can have a huge effect on life expectancy.

- **Sad.** Depression is common in patients with conditions such as chronic kidney disease.

Poor answer A poor answer may include:

- **Less able to travel.** It is difficult to leave the country as portable home dialysis is not always sufficient for certain patients.

- **Unable to work full-time.** It can be difficult to manage employment, as you are spending large chunks of your week in renal dialysis.

- **Fluctuations.** In between dialysis sessions, you can start to feel weak, especially when its been 1-2 days since your last one.

This man is on renal dialysis. He needs to go to the renal centre 3 times a week for 4 hours each time.

What are the challenges of healthcare in rural places? (Part 2 of 2)

Good answer A good answer may include:

- **Physical distance.** There is an issue with access, due to the large distance between patients and services.

- **Isolation.** Many people are isolated, so medical emergencies may not be reported, especially if someone is living alone.

- **Attitudes.** There may be differences in attitudes towards healthcare - e.g. people are less likely to go to see their GP.

- **Lack of doctors.** Some doctors do not want to work in rural areas, as it could be far from home, and it could involve fewer career progression opportunities.

- **Less technology.** Hospitals in rural areas tend to have more basic technology.

MMI Station: Challenges for People

Station Brief: As a doctor, it is important to understand people of different ages.

What social difficulties might children in the 11-15 year old range face? (Part 1 of 2)

Good answer A good answer may include:

- **Moving schools.** It can be an emotional and difficult thing to move schools.

- **Moving house / country.** Many children find it difficult to move house / country.

- **Adolescence.** Teenagers go through many physical and mental changes, which can be difficult.

- **Exam pressure.** Teenagers are faced with the challenges of GCSE and career choices.

- **Social pressures.** Bullying is common, and there are many social pressures present.

- **Mental health.** Although young, teenagers can often go through depression or have things like eating disorders.

As a doctor, it is important to understand people of different ages.

What challenges might a Brighton and Sussex university student (any subject) face in their first term at university? (Part 2 of 2)

Good answer A good answer may include:

- **Making friends** - Freshers can be quite socially difficult. You meet to many new people, and people feel under pressure to make friends.

- **Independent learning** - unlike school, you aren't spoon-fed at university. It varies from course to course, but in medicine you go straight into a 200 person lecture theatre in many universities.

- **New home** - as well as a new 'school', you are likely to be living in a new home. Learning to cook, wash your clothes and do other chores can be a challenge.

- **Tired** - it can be tiring to go out and meet so many people in Freshers, combined with the difficulties of starting a new course.

MMI Station: GP Referral

Station Brief: You are a GP. A 35 year old heavy smoker comes into your practice who has experienced weight loss and has been coughing up blood. What questions would you ask him?

Would you refer him to a specialist, and if so what specialist? What do you know about what doctors do when they send an 'urgent referral'?

Good answer A good answer may include:

- **About his symptoms.** Find out as much as possible about the weight loss and coughing up blood.

- **Related medical issues.** Does he have any other problems currently alongside?

- **Past medical history.** Find out about his past medical history, his lifestyle habits

  (smoking etc.), his family history (genetic aspect).

- **Medication.** Find out about the medication he is taking or has been taking.

- **Depends on severity.** If the issues are very extreme (i.e. lots of weight loss and blood), then it may be worth referring.

- **Symptoms and history.** If his symptoms and history suggest a deeper issue, then referral is useful.

- **Maybe don't refer!** If the patient has explainable short-term issues, you can prescribe him some drugs and only refer if the issues persist in a weeks time.

- **Lungs.** He is coughing out blood, so it may be to do with a lung infection.

- **Dietician.** It may also be useful to refer him to a dietician to monitor his diet and control the weight loss.

- **Refer on to a specialist.** The doctor may have a suspicion about the condition, and would refer the patient on to a specialist.

- **Only some cases need 'urgent' referrals.** For example, if someone has a mini-stroke (transient ischaemic attack), you may refer on for an urgent clinic if you feel the patient is at risk of a second stroke soon.

- **May ask for scans.** The doctor may ask for an urgent type of blood test or scan.

Poor answer A poor answer may include:

- **Asking close ended questions.** You want the questions to be as open as possible to enable you to get as much information as possible.

- **Not asking about past medical history.** You need to do more than just focusing on the blood coughing and weight loss. You need to delve deeper to find out about this patient's history and medication.

- **Refer too easily.** Some may say it is 'safer to refer no matter what'. This is a safe option - yes - but it is unrealistic. The NHS is limited in resources, so the patient should only be referred if he really does need specialist treatment.

- **Illogical specialty.** The student is not expected to have much perquisite medical knowledge. This question is trying to test their logical thinking. Therefore there could be many correct answers for this question. However, if they say they would refer to a podiatrist (foot specialist), then this would seem quite odd.

MMI Station: Picture Description

Station Brief: Please describe this image to the examiner and they will draw it for you. They have not seen it, so you need to be as descriptive as possible. They do not understand the term stick person or the names of body parts. When the image is presented, explain to them what they need to change. Assess its accuracy and give the examiner some feedback on how well they did. **(Part 1 of 2)**

Good answer A good answer may include:

- **Describing step by step.** A good answer may ask the examiner to draw a circle, and then draw a two smaller circles inside, one in the top left quadrant, one in the top right quadrant. And so on….

Poor answer A poor answer may include:

- **Not being specific enough.** For example, for the eyes, you cannot just say 'draw two circles' without specifying where in the big circle (face) they are!

- **Using body parts.** The question clearly says that the examiner does not understand body parts, so don't say 'draw two eyes'.

What is the importance of being able to provide a concise verbal account as a doctor? **(Part 2 of 2)**

Good answer A good answer may include:

- **Important for summaries.** If you examine or consult a patient, you may need to summarise the findings to your team. You can't spend 30 minutes telling the team everything, so you need to be concise.

- **Explaining things to patients.** If a patient is having a treatment, you need to explain concisely and simply how the treatment works. You might have 100s of scientific facts that you can tell the patient, but you need to prioritise.

- **Time pressures.** Doctors are always under time pressure, so providing a concise account is very important. You can link this to things you saw at work experience - e,g. A GP under pressure to do   an   appointment   every   10   minutes.

MMI Station: Neighbour Conversation

Station Brief: Your neighbour is worried about her upcoming hospital appointment. Her husband died 6 months ago from cancer and she is having investigations relating to a potential tumour. **Explore the situation with her and try to deal with her concerns.**

Good answer A good answer may include:

- **Be supportive.** Listen to her and support her. If she becomes emotional, stay calm and composed.

- **Try to improve her mood.** She may start talking about life being pointless without her husband, but you should try to steer the conversation to more positive waters - e.g. talk to her about what she enjoys in life, and make her feel positive and look forward to something.

- **Manage her expectations.** You can't promise her that she hasn't got cancer, but you want to remind her that nothing is diagnosed yet. Even if it is a tumour, the doctors can start chemotherapy.

Poor answer A poor answer may include:

- **Getting uncomfortable.** The station is really testing your ability to comfort someone and provide advice. It is important for you to remain calm and provide useful advice.

- **Upsetting her.** A bad candidate might scare her more about her cancer, which is the opposite of what you need to do.

- **Create unrealistic expectations.** Other candidates go to the other end of the spectrum and promise that there won't be a cancer.

MMI Station: Waiting Room

Station Brief: There is a man sitting in the waiting room, waiting to be called in for his job interview. **Have a conversation with him, calming his nerves before it starts.**

Good answer A good answer may include:

- **Motivate him.** Try to improve his self-esteem and improve his confidence.
- **Give him interview tips.** Give him some simple interview tips, such as structuring his answers, remaining   calm   etc.

- **Empathise.** Show empathy, you can relate to preparing for an interview!

- Stay calm and composed. Make sure you remain composed despite the emotional state of the man.

Poor answer A poor answer may include:

- **Become flustered.** Being affected by the man's emotional state.

- **Become frustrated.** Becoming frustrated at the man's lack of confidence.

- **Failure to motivate him.** Lacking any passion and desire to actually improve his mentality.

- **Failing to empathise.** Failing to relate this to your own situation in an interview - you have to empathise at this station. At the very least you should sympathise.

MMI Station: GP Consultation

Station Brief: Watch the first minute of this short video of a patient taking a history.

How do you think they did and what could they improve on? (Part 1 of 2)

What did she do badly?

- **Poor welcoming.** Not even saying hello in a warm fashion, plus making the patient feel bad for coming back in.

- **Poor tone.** Being very rude to the patient and continually interrupting.

- **Being rude.** Saying that the patient is over-reacting.

- **Being patronising.** She is being patronising, and acting like the patient's parent!

What could she improve on?

- **Warmer tone.** Being nicer to the patient, making them feel at ease.

- **Understanding.** Being more understanding of the patient's struggles rather than arguing.

- **Explaining different options.** Not forcing the patient down a certain route, but instead being receptive and informative.

- **Less forceful.** The doctor came across as passive aggressive here! A GP needs to be efficient, quick   whilst   remaining   kind.

We will now do a role play of the same scenario. You are the GP, and are speaking to the lady, who has just come in. She is tired of taking antibiotics, although she hasn't completed her course. She wants a hysterectomy (surgical removal of the uterus) which would mean she couldn't have children in the future. **Discuss her situation. (Part 2 of 2)**

Good answer A good answer may include:

- **Understand the issue of antibiotics.** In a kind fashion, try to understand why the patient doesn't like taking antibiotics, and find out if they have been beneficial at all.

- **Emphasise the importance of finishing the course of antibiotics.** It is important to finish the antibiotics to prevent increased risk of antibiotic resistance.

- **Discuss hysterectomy.** Make sure the patient is aware they cannot have children in the future.

Poor answer A poor answer may include:

- **Fail to address the issue of antibiotic resistance.** Ignore this issue without even advising the patient to stay on antibiotics.

- **Not attempt to persuade the patient to continue antibiotics.** The patient is frustrated, and clearly wants a quick-fix solution. You cannot force her, but you can warmly explain the benefits of antibiotics to help improve her patience with her current treatment plan.

MMI Station: Making Mistakes

Station Brief: A girl has designed the logo for the university's new gym, and has won a special scholarship for it. She feels she doesn't deserve it, because her brother helped her who is a professional graphic designer. Please comfort her. **(Part 1 of 2)**

Good answer A good answer may include:

- **Stay calm and composed.** Ensure that you provide a calming and reassuring presence to the girl.

- **Explain that she was wrong.** Kindly explain that she was wrong, but don't go too hard. She should be honest and tell the university.

- **Empathise.** Explain that everyone makes mistakes - e.g. you could use an example of when you made a bad mistake.

- **Inspire her.** She could learn from her brother and then design herself in the future.

Poor answer A poor answer may include:

- **Blame the girl.** Lecture her about why she was wrong. It is important to touch on it, but it is clear that the girl already knows she is wrong.

- **Tell her she did nothing wrong.** Whilst its important not to be too hard on her, at the same time you should not advocate this kind of behaviour as it is technically cheating.

- **Become flustered.** Become awkward when the girl becomes emotional and upset.

Tell me about a time you failed. What is resilience? How have you shown this quality? **(Part 2 of 2)**

Good answer A good answer may include:

- **Structured response.** Giving enough detail and explaining in a structured manner.

- **An actual failure.** Some students tend to be scared to talk about a real failure.

- **Reflecting on what you learnt.** Explaining how you learnt from your failure, and why you were resilient.

- **Ideally linking resilience into the same example.** It would be ideal to use the example of failure to explain how you showed resilience.

Poor answer A poor answer may include:

- **Not giving a real failure.** For example, saying 'I only managed to raise £10,000 for charity when my aim was £12,000' isn't the best response. They want to hear about when you actually failed and what you did.

- **Misunderstanding resilience.** Resilience is the ability to keep going with your head up, despite challenges and failures. If you don't understand the word, ask for clarification rather than answering wrongly!

MMI Station: Dietician Scenario

Station Brief: You are the **dietician** and you are going to all the patients asking them what they would like to have for dinner. You reach a patient who is wearing a headscarf and you would like to find out if they eat Halal meat. However, they cannot speak English and tell you to speak to their friend. You are on the phone to the friend of the patient who is angrily refusing to provide any information and is demanding information on the patient's condition. **Please talk to him, trying to resolve the situation.**

Good answer A good answer may include:

- **Stay calm and composed.** As always, in role plays you have to remain calm.

- **Try to find out the information.** Try to find out about the patient's diet preference, but don't push too hard - you can always serve vegetarian food.

- **Respect patient confidentiality.** The friend is not necessarily related, so you have to refuse to disclose any details.

Poor answer A poor answer may include:

- **Become frustrated.** You cannot just stop talking to the friend, as this is rude.

- **Not try to discern the dietary information.** As a dietician, it is useful to find out what the patient can eat. If they do eat meat, then its useful to eat meat to gain protein and iron (as opposed to just giving them a vegetarian meal by default).

MMI Station: NHS and Complaints

Station Brief: Your mother, Clarissa, has been given the wrong insulin dose by the doctors. You are now seeing the doctor to complain about what has happened. **Please talk to them about what has happened. (Part 1 of 2)**

Good answer A good answer may include:

- **Talk calmly with respect.** You want to complain, but not in a rude fashion. You need to maintain respect for the doctors.

- **Find out more information.** Try to find out the reason why the insulin dose was wrong.

- **How will the mistake be avoided in future?** Find out how they aim to improve and learn.

- **Ask about complaints process.** Ask about the process by which you can file an official complaint.

- **Clarissa's future care.** Find out the impact on Clarissa's health, and ask about her future treatment.

- **Make it diabetes specific.** It is useful to reference in questions related to diabetes. Ask about Clarissa's glucose levels, ask whether it was an over-dose or under-dose. Show an awareness for the specific situation in hand.

- **Push doctors to improve.** Complaints keep the NHS on its toes. They ensure that doctors do not get away with mistakes, and are under pressure to perform.

- **Give patients a voice.** If there was not a complaints process, then patients would feel stifled and feel   as   if   they   have   no   voice.

- **Useful when big mistakes are made.** A patient's family will understandably be angry if a big mistake is made, and they have the right to complain.

- **Can identify poor care.** If a doctor is providing a poor quality of care, whether this is through carelessness or due to another reason, then complaints can help catch them and identify the issue.

Why are complaints vital to the functioning of the NHS? What do you know about the complaints process? **(Part 2 of 2)**

Good answer A good answer may include:

- **You can discuss a complaint with the Patient Advice and Liason Service (PALS).** Some people find it helpful to talk to someone who understands the complaints process first and get some guidance and support. You'll find a Patient Advice and Liaison Service (PALS) in most hospitals.

- **You can complain directly to an NHS service provider.** You can complain directly to a

  GP, a dentist surgery, a hospital etc.

- **Or you can complain to the commissioner of services.** This is body that pays for the NHS services you use. You should complain within 12 months of the incident.

- **You receive a written response.** Once the complaint has been investigated, the complainer receive a written response. The response should set out the findings and, where appropriate, provide apologies and information about what's being done as a result of the complaint.

MMI Station: Confused Older Women

Station Brief: You are a current medical student at Manchester, and you are crossing the road and you see an elderly woman who is confused and looks lost. **Please speak to her and answer her questions. (Part 1 of 2)**

Good answer A good answer may include:

- **Remain calm -** you need to provide a calming and composed presence.

- **Have a chat - she may just want** someone to talk to, to help her cheer up.

- **Find out where she's going -** she looks lost, so help guide her on her path home.

- **Motivate her -** when she becomes upset and loses confidence, motivate her and try to improve her outlook on life.

Poor   answer   A   poor   answer   may   include:

- **Ignore her emotions -** some candidates become awkward and try to ignore the emotional parts of this station.

- **Be too brash -** if the elderly lady is losing happiness, don't go straight into encouraging her to be happy again. She has lost her husband, so you need to show a degree of empathy, and then gently try to lift her mood.

You are a current medical student at Manchester, and you are crossing the road and you see an elderly woman who is confused and looks lost. **For the next part, imagine she has fallen over and you are helping her. (Part 2 of 2)**

Good answer A good answer may include:

- **Help her up -** offer to help her up (even though its not an action station!)

- **Refer to A&E -** as she is elderly she probably needs to go get a check-up urgently.

- **Console her further -** you need to continue motivating and supporting her.

- **Offer to help her home -** offer to call her a taxi, or walk her to her destination, or take her to A&E. Find out if she has a carer

- **DRABCDE.** Take a DRABCDE approach (e.g. Make sure there is no danger nearby and check if she is still awake and she can hear you)

- **Make her comfortable.** Making her feel comfortable and safe. Reassure her that help is on the way and that she will be brought back to safety.

Poor answer A poor answer may include:

- **Letting her leave -** you shouldn't let her walk off alone after finding out that she is elderly, upset and physically unstable

- **Not consoling her -** you may continue to be poor at consoling and motivating her

- **Undermining her -** saying things like 'you shouldn't walk from now on' or 'you need a wheelchair now' could be taken as offensive. She may be able to walk normally, but has had a one-off fall.

- **Bombarding her -** bombarding her with lots of questions!

Examiner's Tip - You must call for help in any emergency situation, and this is a core value all medical students are taught - You are not expected to know this but you can impress the interviewers with this and   will   show   that   you   are   using   your   initiative.

MMI Station: Injured Cyclist

Station Brief: You are a Manchester Medical Student on a placement in A&E. You have been asked to speak to a cyclist who has had a fall.

Ask them what happened, if they are in any pain and reassure them in case they are distressed. In the second part of the station, you will need to present your findings to an A&E doctor. **(Part 1 of 2)**

Good answer A good answer may include:

- **Ask for the chain of events.** First of all, it is good to get a chain of events. What happened, in what order, and why?

- **Ask about the pain.** Be specific when asking about the pain - where is it, what kind of pain (e.g. throbbing, in a particular place?).

- **Ask about past medical history.** It is important to know more about this patient - e.g.

  is he a diabetic, has he got asthma?

- **Be calming.** Ensure you support them.

Poor answer A poor answer may include:

- **Asking close ended questions.** It is useful to ask open ended questions to try to get as much information as possible from the patient.

- **Forgetting to reassure the patient.** Many candidates get caught up in the process of finding out information, and forget to reassure and comfort the patient who is clearly distressed.

You are a Manchester Medical Student on a placement in A&E. You have been asked to speak to a cyclist who has had a fall.

Summarise your findings to Dr. Iqbal, the A&E consultant. (Part 2 of 2)

Good answer A good answer may include:

- **Summarise concisely.** Do not tell the doctor every single detail. Pick out the important facts.

- **Prioritise.** It is useful to focus on the important details first - e.g. the patient is diabetic, has ankle and thigh pain which they graded 4/5 (its a good idea to ask for a grade!)

- **Structure.** A good structure is to talk about the presentation, then the past medical history and (if appropriate) lifestyle factors / family history.

Example Response

This is a 24 year old male, who has had an accident involving falling off their bicycle. They fell sideways after hitting a bump in the road.

The main problem is a pain in the lower half of the body, which is particularly strong in the left ankle and left thigh. The patient graded the pain as 4/5.

The patient is conscious and is otherwise seemingly well. The man is a Type 1 diabetic, but has no other past medical history.

MMI Station: MedSoc Speech Nerves

Station Brief: You are vice-president of your school Medical Society. You have won an award for the best medical society in the UK. Your president is due to give a speech and is nervous and doesn't want to now go on stage. **Please talk to her to find out why she is nervous and reassure her.**

Good answer A good answer may include:

- **Calm her down.** Don't be too frantic, and stay calm and composed.

- **Motivate her.** Keep telling her that she will do a great job, and try to improve her confidence.

- **Inspire her.** She has just led the medical society to an amazing award, she should be proud and should enjoy the moment.

- **Discuss the speech content.** Give her ideas for the speech - if she has some content she may feel calmer.

Poor answer A poor answer may include:

- **Agreeing to replace her.** The task is so calm her down and reassure her. You shouldn't jump at the opportunity to do the speech if she offers.

- **Becoming flustered.** Stay calm, and don't get flustered if she becomes emotional.

- **Not finding out why she is nervous.** Many candidates begin straight away reassuring, without actually finding out why she is nervous. Is it because she hasn't written a content? Is she nervous of her voice? Is she nervous of the number of people?

MMI Station: Fictitious Friend

Station Brief: Your friend Julio has had a dog for over 6 years. Unfortunately, it is very ill and needs to be put down, but Julio is very reluctant. What would you say to your friend? What solutions would you offer? Julio has come to you for advice.

Good answer A good answer may include:

- **Sympathising with Julio.** In this station it is very important to show sympathy and empathise with Julio.

- **Spin a positive angle.** Try to make him celebrate Julio's life, rather than look at his passing as as sad thing.

- **Help him move on.** You could suggest helping him find a new dog, but you don't want to offend him, so be careful with this.

- **Being supportive.** Be kind and be there for him.

Poor answer A poor answer may include:

- **Getting flustered.** Becoming flustered when Julio becomes emotional.

- **Not supporting.** Not being friendly enough, and instead being overly corporate and methodological. You are meant to be a friend, not a doctor.

- **Offending Julio.** Don't downplay the importance of the dog's passing. This might offend Julio.

MMI Station: Role Play: Concert Latecomer

Station Brief: You are a steward at a concert and someone has arrived 10 minutes later than the final entry time. They are not allowed in and have travelled from a different country to get here. **Please explain this to the fan. (Part 1 of 2)**

Good answer A good answer may include:

- **Stand firm.** You have to stick by the policy of the concert, otherwise you may lose your job.

- **Be firm but consoling.** The person is distressed, so you cannot be too harsh. Find a balance between being nice and being authoritative.

- **Suggest solutions.** Try to suggest alternatives - e.g. buy a ticket for a different concert, do other great things in the city, enjoy your evening doing something else.

- **Adapt.** When the person is angry, remain firm. When the person is sad, show sympathy.

Poor   answer   A   poor   answer   may   include:

- **Letting him in.** This is betraying the policy of the concert venue, and you are likely to lose your job.

- **Being too cold.** Do not be overly cold. This could cause the person to become aggressive.

- **Simply say 'sorry'.** There needs to be progression to this station. You cannot just keep saying 'sorry I cannot let you in'. You need to console the patient, suggest alternatives and engage.

Evaluate your performance. How do you think you did? What would you improve? **(Part 2 of 2)**

Good answer A good answer may include:

- **Talk through your thinking.** This is a good opportunity to explain why you did different things.

  - e.g. I tried to find a balance between being kind and also being authoritative

  - E.g. I decided to stand more firm when he was aggressive, as I did not want him to think I was weak or persuadable.

- **Think of improvements.** It can be difficult to critique yourself immediately, but try not to just be positive!

MMI Station: Difficult Communication

Station Brief: You are a junior doctor and you need to give a vaccination to Lossy, a 6 year old girl. She is scared of needles and starts crying. The consultant and mother both tell you to give her the vaccination even though Lossy is refusing. **What are some of the issues raised here? (Part 1 of 3)**

Good answer A good answer may include:

- **Autonomy.** Autonomy means respecting a patient's ability to make decisions. People have a right to decide about their own healthcare.

- **Competency.** However, the patient is 6 years old, so it is unlikely that they are competent to make their own decisions. You can do a Gillick competency test (see link before). If the patient is Gillick competent, this situation can be escalated. Otherwise, the doctor can listen to the mother and do the vaccination.

- **Address Lossy's concerns.** Before jumping to any debates about competence, it is best to calm Lossy down. Give her a lollipop, ask her why she is scared, and explain the importance of the vaccination. You can even arrange another appointment another time, as Lossy may be feeling particularly scared today.

Lossy returns a year later and now needs to have a lumbar puncture which carries a small risk of spinal cord paralysis. This time Lossy is accompanied by her father and her father says that he will blame you personally if the lumbar puncture goes wrong. **How would you react in this situation? (Part 2 of 3)**

Good answer A good answer may include:

- **Stay calm and composed.** Although it can be easy to become pressured, the best thing for a doctor to do is remain calm and focus on the task ahead.

- **Explain the risks.** It is best to be open and explain the risks of the procedure. Also explain exactly what you are doing, because if the father understands the process, he may be more understanding.

- **Explain why the lumbar puncture is done.** Explain the importance of the lumbar puncture. The father can then decide if he wants it to be done.

- **Refer on to a consultant.** If you still feel inexperienced with the lumbar puncture process, then you could ask someone more experienced to do this specific procedure. Although you have to learn to become comfortable, a pressurised situation is not an ideal learning curve!

You find out that Lossy's parents divorced when Lossy was 2 years old. **How do you think this has affected the relationship she has had with her family? (Part 3 of 3)**

Good answer A good answer may include:

- **She may be more distant.** She may be less close to each of her parents.

- **She may be closer to one parent.** Lossy may be more close to one parent. If they disagree on her treatment, it could be a difficult situation, especially if Lossy is regarded as non-competent.

- **She may have had a difficult upbringing.** It can be tough when parents get divorced. We should not assume, but Lossy may have grown up in an environment filled with arguing and conflict.

MMI Station: Change in Medication

Station Brief: A 16 year old patient has a medication change in their morphine. There is a change from subcutaneous injections to oral forms of morphine. You normally need to multiply the dose by 2.1. Morphine comes in oral tablets of 20mg only. The subcutaneous dose was 30mg. **Please explain to Alex how many tablets they have to take a day and how you came to this calculation? (Part 1 of 2)**

Good answer A good answer may include:

- **Explaining simply.** You need to speak in laymen terms so that Alex can understand.

- **Re-assure him of safety.** Ensure that he is aware that oral forms of morphine are just as safe, and make sure he is calm about his new treatment.

- **Alex requires 3 tablets.** Ideally we need to give 63mg of morphine. However, we only have tablets of 20mg. It is not a good idea to give too much morphine, so 60mg is better than 80mg.

Poor answer A poor answer may include:

- **Speaking too medically.** Using overly scientific or mathematical terms may confuse the 16 year old patient.

- **Incorrect calculation.** Some students may make a mistake with the actual calculation.

- **Giving 4 tablets.** It is not safe to give 80mg - this would be an overdose. It is better to round down to 60mg from 63mg

Alex is scared of needles and so oral-dentistry is a better alternative for him. **What are some of the reasons patients are not compliant with their dentistry? (Part 2 of 2)**

Good answer A good answer may include:

- **Scared of needles.** A common reason is because patients are scared of needles.

- **Side effects.** Certain drugs can have unwanted side effects (e.g. weight gain) that

  patients do not want.

- **Ethical reasons.** Some treatments, like gene therapy, have ethical issues associated with them, which leads to some patients declining.

- Length. Some patients want a quicker fix, so may decline the recommended dentistry.

- **Social beliefs.** Some patients read articles about certain treatments, which can lead to a preference for an uncommon treatment.

MMI Station: Drug Calculation

Station Brief: You are a Manchester Medical Student.You are a Manchester Medical Student. The consultant has asked you to do a calculation. A patient, Jessica, is currently on an IVI drip. She needs to receive 1000ml using a controller with a drip factor of 15 drops/ml. The infusion begins at 1pm, although the patient needs to have a 30 minute rest every four hours. The drip rate is 20 drops per minute.

Calculate the volume of liquid left at 6pm.

Good answer A good answer may include:

Break the information down:

There are 15 drops per ml. So the rate of 20 drops / minute is the equivalent to 1.333 ml / minute. This is equivalent to 1.333 x 60 ml / hour, which is 80 ml / hour.

Between 1pm and 6pm there are 5 hours. However, we have a 30 minute break, so there are actually only 4.5 hours of drip time.

4.5 x 80ml = 360ml of drip given. Therefore there is 1000 - 360 left = **640ml**

Personality

MMI Station: Personal Qualities

Station Brief: This station will focus on personal qualities.

Tell me about a time you failed. What is resilience? How have you shown this quality? (Part 1 of 3)

Good answer A good answer may include:

- Structured response. Giving enough detail and explaining in a structured manner.

- An actual failure. Some students tend to be scared to talk about a real failure.

- Reflecting on what you learnt. Explaining how you learnt from your failure, and why you were resilient.

- Ideally linking resilience into the same example. It would be ideal to use the example of failure to explain how you showed resilience.

Poor answer A poor answer may include:

- **Not giving a real failure.** For example, saying 'I only managed to raise £10,000 for charity when my aim was £12,000' isn't the best response. They want to hear about when you actually failed and what you did.

- **Misunderstanding resilience.** Resilience is the ability to keep going with your head up, despite challenges and failures. If you don't understand the word, ask for clarification rather than answering wrongly!

This station will focus on personal qualities.

What does integrity mean? How do you ensure a sense of trust? (Part 2 of 3)

Good answer A good answer may include:

- **Integrity** is the quality of being honest and showing good moral principles.

- **Give an example.** For example, a doctor being honest to his patients and respecting their confidentiality is an example of integrity.

- **You can gain trust with integrity.** You can obtain trust by acting kindly, showing honesty and supporting others around you.

This station will focus on personal qualities.

Give me a situation on where you have used teamwork? What makes you a good team member? Why is teamwork important? (Part 3 of 3)

Good answer A good answer may include:

Give me a situation on where you have used teamwork?

- Structured response. Giving enough detail and explaining in a structured manner.

- Explaining how you demonstrated teamwork. Rather than just describing when you worked in a team, explain how you worked together.

What makes you a good team member?

- Work hard - do your allocated tasks efficiently and well

- Approachable - a point of support for others

- Listen well - easy to work with, and take on board other team members' ideas

- Flexible - even if you do not agree with the decision, you adapt for the good of the team

- Communication - relay information back to the team about your tasks, and contribute ideas.

Why is teamwork important?

- **Delegation of tasks -** each person can specialise

- **Combining expertise -** pool together ideas

- **Reducing individual workload -** can share work out

- **Increased motivation -** keep each other going

- **e.g. Multidisciplinary Team -** give example of MD team in surgical work experience

MMI Station: Candidate as a Person

Station Brief: Studying medicine can be intense, so maintaining a work-life balance is important.

How do you relax and unwind? (Part 1 of 2)

Good answer A good answer may include:

- **Extracurricular activities.** Link in things like charity work, socialising with friends, reading and playing music instruments.

- **Explain how you maintain stress.** Touch on how you reduce stress, e.g. by keeping a diary, making lists, remaining organised.

Poor answer A poor answer may include:

- **Simplistic activities.** Even though you might watch TV to unwind, don't mention this as the main thing. Try to be a bit cultural or academic!

- **Being overly academic.** If you say you read research papers on genetics as a hobby, this might sound odd. It could be true, but they are trying to find out that you're more than just an academic person.

Examiner's Tip - Universities want someone more than just an academic person. They want someone who will come to university, interact with others, join in societies, show leadership and really contribute to the university community. So don't shy away from showing your personality.

Medical students are selected from the best and the brightest students around the world. How will you cope with moving from an environment where you were one of the best students to one where everyone has a similar level of ability? **(Part 2 of 2)**

Good answer A good answer may include:

- **Its a challenge!** e.g. it will push me to be even better and work harder! I like a challenge.

- **I can learn from others.** I would love to learn and bounce of others in discussions and tutorials.

Poor answer A poor answer may include:

- **I will hate it.** Don't say that you'll absolutely hate it! Because thats the reality.

- **Show defeat.** At the same time, don't accept you'll be bottom of the class. Show some drive, passion and determination to be as good as you can possibly be!

MMI Station: Leadership and Teamwork

Station Brief:

1. How have you shown leadership skills?

2. Can you tell me why team-working abilities are important for doctors?

3. What qualities are needed in a good teammate?

Good answer A good answer may include:

1. How have you shown leadership skills?

- **Structure to answer.** Structure your answer properly, explaining the role of leadership. STARR is a good structure. The example could be, for example, being captain of a sports team, leading a school society etc.

- **Explain why you were a leader.** Explain what you did to show leadership. Did you remain a good listener, taking on board feedback from everyone in the team? Did you allocate tasks well? Did you maintain a good balance between authority and remaining kind?

- **Discuss what type of leader you are.** Everyone is a different leader. Some people are authoritative all the time. Some people are quiet, and earn respect of their team as a leader.

2. Can you tell me why team-working abilities are important for doctors?

- **Multidisciplinary teams.** Doctors often have to work in MDTs. For example, a surgeon might work with nurses, GPs, anaesthetists, physiotherapists, occupational therapists.

- **Transfer between shifts.** A key part of teamwork is transferring between shifts. When one doctor leaves, they need to pass on the key info to the incoming doctor. There needs to be co-operation, understanding and teamwork!

- **Important to respect team members.** In the stressful environment of medicine, it is important to respect those working in your team. If you have poor team-working abilities, you are less likely to succeed. For example, a humble consultant who appreciates the fantastic work done by nurses is much, much better than an arrogant consultant who dismisses nurses as less important members of his team.

3. What qualities are needed in a good teammate?

- **Work hard -** do your allocated tasks efficiently and well

- **Approachable -** a point of support for others

- **Listen well -** easy to work with, and take on board other team members' ideas

- **Flexible -** even if you do not agree with the decision, you adapt for the good of the team

- **Communication -** relay information back to the team about your tasks, and contribute ideas.

MMI Station: Teamwork

Station Brief: During your time at Leeds, you will often have to work in small teams, whether it be in group-learning tutorials, or in a hospital ward in later years.

Explain why each of these 4 skills are important in medicine: **(Part 1 of 2)**

- Teamwork

- Leadership

- Communication

- Organisation

Good answer A good answer may include:

- **Teamwork** is important as a doctor when you work in multidisciplinary teams, such as in surgery where you work with anaesthetists, nurses and other clinicians.

- **Leadership** is important as a doctor as you need to manage multidisciplinary teams, and show leadership to both the patient and colleagues.

- **Communication** is essential to build a doctor patient relationship. You have to be able to talk to patients, especially when breaking bad news, taking a history, explaining a treatment etc.

- **Organisation** is key for managing time with tasks. Doctors are often under time pressure, so it is important to be organised and efficient.

What makes key skills make someone a good team member? **(Part 2 of 2)**

Good answer A good answer may include:

- **Work hard -** do your allocated tasks efficiently and well

- **Approachable -** a point of support for others

- **Listen well -** easy to work with, and take on board other team members' ideas

- **Flexible -** even if you do not agree with the decision, you adapt for the good of the team

- **Communication -** relay information back to the team about your tasks, and contribute ideas.

MMI Station: Free Time

Station Brief: At your time at UEA medical school, you will have to work very hard, and even harder when you qualify as a doctor. This station will discuss stress and relaxation.

What do you do in your free time? Do you have any hobbies? (Part 1 of 2)

Good answer A good answer may include:

- **Be honest.** Speak honestly about what you do to enjoy yourself. Don't be overly academic and force a 'fake' answer.

- **Seem creative.** It is better to pick something creative, such as charity fundraising or running, rather than saying you enjoy watching TV.

- **Explain how it helps you.** Don't just describe the activity - explain how it helps you de-stress and also why you actually enjoy it!.

Poor answer A poor answer may include:

- **Being too simplistic.** Saying you enjoy watching TV may be honest, but it can come across as simplistic.

- **Being overly academic.** Some students try too hard to be academic - e.g. they say that they enjoy reading research papers on medicine in their spare time. They want to make sure that you have a way of de-stressing alongside your academia, so show them that you are an all-rounded person who is capable of enjoying themselves and having some down time!

At your time at UEA medical school, you will have to work very hard, and even harder when you qualify as a doctor. This station will discuss stress and relaxation.

Why might you experience stress as a doctor? (Part 2 of 2)

Good answer A good answer may include:

- **Dealing with bad news -** giving bad news to patients can be quite difficult
- **Setbacks -** e.g. if a patient dies, it can be difficult to cope with
- **Time pressures -** relate to your work experience, e.g. in GP you may have seen how stressful it is to manage a different patient every 10 minutes whilst still providing a high quality of care
- **Constant learning -** although exciting, it can be stressful to continuously have to learn and evolve
- **Hospital setting -** seeing so many people and standing around all day can be quite stressful
- **Lack of resources -** there may not be enough staff members, hospital beds or funding in the NHS
- **Difficult patients -** some patients may be rude, some may sue you
- **Long hours -** hours can be quite difficult, especially in FY1 and FY2 where you may have night shifts

MMI Station: Attitudes and Values

Station Brief: Tell me about a time when you have made a positive impact on someone else's life. **(Part 1 of 2)**

Good answer A good answer may include:

- **Structure.** Use the STARR method, or at the very least have some structure to your answer.
- **Describe your impact.** It could be motivating someone to do something, or consoling someone with a problem. Ideally the impact is more than just one conversation.

Poor answer A poor answer may include:

- **Minimal impact.** e.g. my mum was upset, so I calmed her down and cooked her food. Compare this to supporting a friend each week going through a tough time!

- **Being too factual.** You need to show empathy and personality in this question. Show that you cared and helped because you wanted to.

Examiner's Tip - Ideally you should have an answer to this kind of question prepared. Make sure to fill in your model answers in the Medic Mind handbook - it is worth preparing scenarios like 'describe a patient you met', 'describe how you've helped someone', 'discuss a scenario where you had a difficult task' and many more!

Based on your work or voluntary experiences, what do you think are the challenges of delivering quality care to patients? How do you think demonstrating respect and dignity impacts on patients? **(Part 2 of 2)**

Challenges to Delivering Quality Care

- **Difficult patients.** Patients can become frustrated and aggressive

- **NHS funding.** Lack of funding in the NHS affects quality of care

- **Constant learning.** Medicine is constantly changing, so its hard to keep up with the best treatments

- **Making mistakes.** Doctors inevitably make mistakes under pressure and when working fast.

Impact of Respect on Patients

- **Improves confidence.** Increases trust and confidence in doctors.

- **Patients are more open.** Patients are less likely to hold back and feel shy, which helps doctors get full information for a diagnosis.

- **Patients feel supported.** Patients see their doctor as a friend, especially in GP where there is continuity of care over the long-term.

MMI Station: Information Processing / Logic

Station Brief: At this station you will be asked to play a round of "20 Questions" to identify an object, creature, event or place that is known to the interviewer. To determine the answer, you must ask the interviewer a series of questions. The interviewer has been instructed to answer only YES or NO to your questions. You may ask up to 20 questions. All questions must be answerable by YES or NO. You are being scored on the logical approach to your questioning, and not on whether you identify the correct answer.

Good answer A good answer may include:

- **Starting with open-ended questions.** Start with open ended questions to try to gain a general idea into the type of word.

- **Being logical in asking.** If you get a lead, don't jump ship and ask a random unrelated question.

Poor answer A poor answer may include:

- **Making too many guesses.** Close to the end, don't start guessing too much. Try to keep as questions as open as possible until you know roughly what the word is.

Examiner's Tip - This station is linked to your ability to diagnose a patient. When diagnosing, you have to ask logical questions to find out what the problem is. In an appointment, you don't want to ask 100 questions and spend 30 minutes when you could have asked 20 questions and spent 5 minutes!

1:1 MEDICINE INTERVIEW TUTORING

 Delivered by current Medicine students, who excelled in the interview themselves

 A personalised 1:1 approach, tailored to your unique needs

 An overall 93.4% success rate, with students improving their performance by an average of 57.3%

EXCLUSIVE OFFER: GET 70% OFF YOUR FIRST LESSON

Book a free consultation today to unlock this offer by visiting www.medicmind.co.uk/interview-tutoring/ or scan the QR code below

MEDICINE INTERVIEW ONLINE COURSE

 100+ tutorials, and 200+ MMI stations , designed by our Medicine interview experts

 Learn how to answer questions on motivation for Medicine, personal skills, work experience, hot topics, and more

 A range of packages available, including a live day of teaching and 1:1 tutoring

GET 10% OFF USING THE CODE 'BOOK10'

Find our more at www.medicmind.co.uk/interview-online-course/ or scan the QR code below

MEDICINE LIVE MMI CIRCUIT

 Written by real MMI examiners, and trusted by schools and the NHS

 Perform 10 live MMI stations yourself, completing a full circuit, and then pair up to observe an additional 10 stations!

 Experience a wide range of stations, covering role plays, medical ethics, NHS hot topics, work experience, and more

GET 10% OFF USING THE CODE 'BOOK10'

Find our more at www.medicmind.co.uk/medicine-mmi-course/ or scan the QR code below

Printed in Great Britain
by Amazon

30029845R00128